Tong Bridge

Graves Clough

Tong Bridge

STREET

Mill
Cotton

LANE

Smiths Buildings

Brick Field

Lower Tong

TONG LAN

Tong Clough

This book has been published
as a Limited Edition
of which this is

Number *167*

A complete list of the original
subscribers is printed at the
back of the book

THE BOOK OF BACUP

Market Street, Bacup, approaching the town centre c1895.

Elgin Street, Bacup, acknowledged since summer 1986 as the shortest street in the world.

THE BOOK OF
BACUP

BY
KEN F. BOWDEN

BARON
MCMXCIV

PUBLISHED BY BARON BIRCH
FOR QUOTES LIMITED OF WHITTLEBURY IN 1994
AND PRODUCED BY
KEY COMPOSITION, SOUTH MIDLANDS LITHOPLATES,
HILLMAN PRINTERS (FROME) LTD, CHENEY & SONS,
AND WBC BOOKBINDERS LTD

© Ken F. Bowden 1994

All rights reserved. No part of this publication may be reproduced, stored in a retrieval system, or transmitted, in any form or by any means, electronic, mechanical, photocopying, recording or otherwise, without the prior permission of Quotes Limited.

Any copy of this book issued by the Publisher as clothbound or as a paperback is sold subject to the condition that it shall not by way of trade or otherwise, be lent, re-sold, hired out or otherwise circulated without the Publisher's prior consent, in any form of binding or cover other than that in which it is published, and without a similar condition including this condition being imposed on a subsequent purchaser.

ISBN 0 86023 507 6

Contents

Acknowledgements	8
Foreword by Janet Anderson MP	9
The Beginnings	10
Through the Kirk Gate	15
On the Right Tracks	24
Threads of Industry	33
How They Lived	44
Three Villages: Weir, Sharneyford, Britannia	51
Bacup's Benefactors	62
Stacksteads	71
Those in Control	82
In Pursuit of Learning	88
War and Hard Times	95
Fun and Games	102
The Last Forty Years	110
Rebuild or Restore?	115
Select Bibliography	127
Index	126
Subscribers	128

Acknowledgements

Interest in Bacup as it used to be has never been greater — as evidenced by pictures displayed in offices, shops, businesses and homes throughout the town. A photograph of a street demolished some twenty years ago, with its uneven cobbles, adorns the dust jacket of a recent novel set in a northern slum in the 1920s.

As Bacup's librarian for nearly thirty years, I have had to deal with local queries of many different kinds, some of which involved quite a bit of enjoyable detective work. Indeed I often had to advise youngsters eager to consult the history of one of Bacup's outlying villages that it was still waiting for someone to write it.

In *The Book of Bacup,* I have attempted to rectify such omissions, as well as taking into account more recent developments. In doing so, I am especially indebted to Mr & Mrs Wolstan J. Whitaker of Winsley Hall for their kind hospitality and permission to photograph and reproduce pictures relating to their Whitaker forebears and the Broadclough Hall estates.

I gladly acknowledge the help of Ben Ashworth, Raymond Knights, Harry O'Neill, and other members of Bacup Natural History Society; John Cannon; Robert Cecil of Hambledon, whose father was the executor of the Maden Holt estates; Sandra Cruise and staff of Whitaker Park Museum, Rawtenstall; John Davies, whose knowledge of local coal mining is unparalleled; Peter Deegan; the late Mrs Maggie Edwards, for several fascinating sessions retelling her memories; Veda Hitchen; the late Alan James; John W. Johnson; Lancashire Record Office; Joyce Marlow, author of books about the Whitworth Family, George I and the Peterloo massacre; Michael J. Onley; Frank Seed and officials of Rossendale Borough Council for facilitating the taking of awkward photographs; John Simpson; Alan Stansfield, for providing several photographs and Baptist material; the late Gordon Taylor whose researches proved invaluable and John B. Taylor, for permission to reproduce several drawings and sketches.

My thanks are also expressed to the following holders of copyright photographs for permission to reproduce: the Imperial War Museum; Roger A. Birch; Eric Bollington; George Clarke; Thomas Hampson; Rev John Hargreaves; Alfred Humberston; Rachel Kenyon; Bill Meller; Neal B. Nuttall and Karen R. Spencer. Thank you also to MP Janet Anderson for her generous Foreword.

I am also grateful to M. J. Dolan, Lancashire County Librarian and my library colleagues at Blackpool, Burnley, and Rawtenstall for their willingness to track down obscure pieces of information and provide relevant material and, in particular, Susan A. Halstead, whose constructive criticism and valuable counsel have gone a long way towards making this book readable.

And last, but by no means least, my thanks go to all those friends in Bacup who have so readily loaned precious photographs, delved into their memories, or offered generous advice on behalf of *The Book of Bacup.*

Any shortcomings are the responsibility of this author alone.

Foreword

by Janet Anderson MP

Ken Bowden's book is a must for all lovers of the Rossendale valley who want to learn more, and an excellent introduction to the history of Bacup for newcomers.

The comprehensive research which Ken Bowden has clearly undertaken should be applauded. The book spans the centuries and encompasses areas as diverse as religion, communications and transport, Bacup's industry, its people and benefactors, education and leisure, how the town survived the war, the depression and much more besides.

Bacup is a small but proud and independent town in the Valley of Rossendale. It has a history which deserves to be written. It has managed to withstand the decline of its traditional industries — the cotton mills and the slipper works — and can deservedly stand tall today.

But the most important aspect of Bacup life is its people. Their warmth and community spirit is second to none. Ken Bowden's work is a testament to that warmth and that spirit.

Read it and you will come to love the people of Bacup and the Rossendale Valley as I have done.

Janet Anderson

Key to Caption Credits

AH	Alfred Humberston	MJO	Michael J. Onley
AS	Alan Stansfield	NBN	Neal B. Nuttall
BL	Bacup Library	PN	Paddy Navin
BNHS	Bacup Natural History Society	RAB	Roger A. Birch
EB	Eric Bollington	RC(1)	Robert Cecil
GC	George Clarke	RC(2)	Robert Caulfield
HO'N	Harry O'Neill	RK	Rachel Kenyon
IWM	Imperial War Museum	RL	Rawtenstall Library
JBT	John B. Taylor	SAH	Susan A. Halstead
JH	Rev John Hargreaves	TH	Thomas Hampson
JWJ	John W. Johnson	WJW	Wolstan J. Whitaker
KRS	Karen R. Spencer	WM	William (Bill) Meller
		WMH	Walter M. Haworth

Christopher Saxton's map of Lancashire 1577, the first one to show Bacup.

The Beginnings

There are those who refer to Bacup, somewhat disparagingly, as the last place God made — and forgot to finish. And even one modern commentator considers 'a visit to it . . . not that enlightening'.

However, Roger de Lacy's charter of 1200, the earliest written record which can be traced, mentions Fulebachope: 'the brook in the shut-in valley'. The first element in the name is derived from the Old English *fūl*, implying that the valley must have been somewhat muddy at that time. References to Bacup appear earlier than either of its Rossendale neighbours, the earliest specific mention of Rawtenstall and Haslingden both being in 1241.

Apart from some flint arrowheads and a Duggleby adze found on local hills, there is little indication of any settlement in the Bacup area before the Saxon era. Although the area was part of the large tribal kingdom of Brigantia, there are no relics of Brigantian influence, nor Roman, nor even Danish, though the Saxons certainly left their mark, the most popular explanation of Bacup's name being that it derives from the Anglo-Saxon *bay* (brown) and *cope* (a hill).

At least 32 sites have been claimed for the Battle of Brunanbur(g)h in the year 937, a battle described as the Waterloo of the 10th century. One of the claimants is Broadclough Dykes, an earthworks to the left of the major road north out of Bacup, which stretches some 600 yards along a gently rising slope between Dykes House Farm and Whitaker Clough. Opinions differ as to whether the Dykes are man-made or a natural formation.

Burnley lies on the river Brun, and Brunanbur(g)h is simply 'a fortification on the river Brun'. Here, the Anglo-Saxon forces under King Athelstan defeated a confederacy of Vikings, Danes and Strathclyde Britons under the command of Anlaf, thus establishing a single kingdom of England. The *Anglo-Saxon Chronicle* records that the battle was fought in a land of hills and moors, frequented by wolves and eagles — both recorded in Rossendale in Saxon times. Short of a full-scale archaeological dig, it may never be possible to *prove* that Bacup possesses the site of one of the great battles of British history, though the discovery in May 1840 of what is now known as the Cuerdale hoard, on the banks of the River Ribble some 30 miles from Bacup, seems to confirm that the Battle of Brunanbur(g)h took place not so far away. There is a tradition that a Danish chieftain was killed in the battle, and his body buried in the vicinity of Lee Farm, Bacup.

130 years later, after the Battle of Hastings, William the Conqueror assigned the densely-wooded Forest of Rossendale and other tracts of land to Roger de Poictou, who established his castle at Lancaster, thereby becoming the first Norman lord of the manor and the first Duke of Lancaster — and, through his great-great-granddaughter Isabella who married King John, a direct ancestor of Queen Elizabeth II.

The Domesday survey of 1085/6 does not mention any Bacup or Rossendale place names, but most of the area formed part of the Hundred of Blackburn, one of the six hundreds into which Lancashire was divided. A 'Hundred' was the name given to a geographical area occupied by a hundred or so families. The Hundred of Salford, which included the parish of Rochdale, came up to the River Irwell on the southern side.

For tne next century, there is little evidence of any dwellings in the Bacup area, which remained basically uncultivated hunting territory where roamed the deer, stags and wolves which subsequently gave their names to local areas. But towards the end of the twelfth century, during the reign of King John, the manorial rights of the area came under the control of the de Lacy family. Roger de Lacy was the Constable of Chester — an important office in Norman society, and deriving from the Latin *comes stabuli* (master of the stable), but which had not yet evolved into its current definition: 'One who keeps the King's Peace'.

The de Lacys assigned part of the Forest of Rossendale to the Cistercian monks who operated from Whalley Abbey, and stressed the importance of manual labour and fieldwork. They introduced many farming improvements and so began the process of cultivation, aided by severe weather conditions, which led to natural deforestation as a result of trees being destroyed by a devastating tornado.

By 1296 the eleven vaccaries (or cow-pastures) in Rossendale included one owned by Alan de Roclif in the Bacup area, which pastured 35 cows, 15 calves, seven steers (one young bull), 16 yearlings (seven males), and six heifers. Their total value was 6s 11½d. Another Bacup vaccary was tenanted by Adam of the Dene, who had 33 head of cattle, and paid 26s 8d in rent, as did his brother Alexander of the Dene for a vaccary at Tunstead. Tax returns on personal property, recorded in 1334, showed that Lancashire was the poorest of all the 38 counties thus assessed.

By now the earliest name assigned to any settlement at the eastern end of the Rossendale Valley was 'Bacup Fold', roughly identical with the present town centre. Here, in 1341-42, it was found necessary to repair the vaccary buildings. Basically, these were crude, timber-built structures with thatched roofs, the homes of families who had lived in the forest a long time. That year a new shed was built at Bacup, comprising two cross-beams each 80 feet long, seven beams, 14 posts, 32 joists or tie-beams, four large sills, 160 boards and a thousand laths — which had to be shaped on the spot ready to be put together. The carpenter was paid 28s for his part of the work, transporting the wood cost 8s, and the spikings and iron nails used to fasten the wood together cost a further two shillings. In true Biblical tradition, the 16 men employed in helping the carpenter to construct the building were each paid one penny for their day's work, while the man who thatched the roof earned 3s 8d.

By now the lordship of the manor had passed to the Crown, which became the largest landowner in the area, but had little personal interest in cattle rearing on remote northern estates. It leased the vaccaries and collected rents from the erstwhile cowkeepers who had now become tenants.

The final clearance of the Forest of Rossendale began in 1504 when land was leased at 4d per acre. By 1507, when Henry VII abolished the forest laws, Rossendale had 25 foresters and 72 copyholders, each with their own smallholding of between 2½ and 6½ acres. The Court Rolls of Clitheroe Castle list 45 copyholders in Bacup who in 1527 paid a total of £11 in rents, two from Rockcliffe Wood who each paid 8s 4d, and 11 from Tunsteed (*sic*) whose rental amounted to £5 12s 0d.

Each of the 28 manors of the Honor of Clitheroe had its own greave, the chief officer or bailiff, whose principal function was to collect rents and taxes. Rossendale's greave was appointed every Michaelmas, elected in rotation from each booth at the Halmot Court. The Court met twice a year, presided over by the deputy steward of the manor, and which all adult males who had lived in the area for a year and a day were supposed to attend — though in practice only the main tenants did so. The Halmot Court functioned until 1925.

Bacup Booth was developing into a hamlet — a cluster of houses at a spot known as 'Giddy Meadow'.

A John Whyttacior of Bacup was one of two overlords appointed either as greave of 'yerdes lokyrys' (herd lookers) in 1519 for Rossendale; his grandson James was Greave of Rossendale in 1559, as was *his* grandson John (who married Agnes, daughter of John Towneley of Hurstwood) 120 years later.

Smallholders were becoming accustomed to divide their land between their sons, so that it gradually became less economic to make a living just from the soil. Agriculture would never become really profitable in Rossendale's damp climate and clayey soil, but the barren uplands were well adapted for the rearing of sheep and so, during the reign of King Henry VIII, the upland farmers turned to the spinning wheel and household loom as a profitable sideline. Thus began the woollen (textile) industry whch rapidly became staple trade, and by 1577 Bacup was on the map — Christopher Saxton's Lancashire.

When the manor of Rochdale was surveyed in 1626, it included the Rossendale Hamlett (*sic*) of Brandwood, which embraced a total of just over 2,542 acres with a value of £257 5s 0d. The landowners were the Holts of Grislehurst, ancestors of the Holts of Stubbylee.

During the 17th century, the population of Bacup reached 200. Records from 1662 confirm that in a rental for six months of that year, 35 Bacup land-holders altogether paid £5 10s 0d, by which time Bacup was being described as a specialist textile manufacturing centre.

But even in 1676, Lancashire in general and Rossendale in particular remained one of the most thinly populated and poorest areas in the country. Bacup had its own village green, Hammerton Green, where the original Bacup Fair was held and travelling pedlars came to sell their wares. Nearby later were the old stocks, originally erected in 1749, and later transferred to the old dungeon at the back of Bacup Fold until they fell into disuse about 1850.

Here the villagers of Bacup could breathe the purest air they could expect to find, while the sparkling lime-free water of an unpolluted River Irwell was second to none. The river itself ran through Bacup Fold and was forded by stepping stones known as Door Stones — later the name of Bacup's best-known lodging house.

The hills of Bacup were alive with the sound of bleating, and the village by now comprised the district of Boston (with its bridge built c1632 and demolished 1895), Hempsteads, and the cottages about Newgate — a small Pennine agricultural community. The local woollen industry took its first tentative steps from home to factory, one being recorded in 1745, thus increasing the scale of production, so that when Bishop Richard Pococke, archdean of Dublin, travelled through England in March 1751, he described Bacup as 'a large village where they have a great manufacture of woollen clothes which they send white to London. They are mostly Presbyterians, and have, as they call them, two chapels'.

Four years later the first major road in East Lancashire helped to put Bacup on the map, a turnpike linking Manchester with Skipton *via* Rochdale, Bacup and Burnley.

ABOVE: Broadclough Hall and estate — a rustic paradise, showing an older building of wood on the current site, c1600. The original painting hangs in Winsley Hall, Shrewsbury. (WJW) BELOW: Broadclough Dykes — a view north of Whitaker Clough.

Through the Kirk Gate

Three large stones jutting out of the wall on the old road from Step Row to Deerplay are part of the old 'Kirk Gate' from Heald across the Broadclough estates and on to Newchurch, a distance of four miles each way.

Until the Reformation Lancashire was a Catholic county — and indeed the church built at Newchurch in 1511 was a Catholic one, known for forty years as 'the chapel of our Saviour in Rossendale'. But Bacup always had a strong nonconformist bias, much of which stemmed from the end of the English Civil War, when Oliver Cromwell disbanded his army at Clitheroe.

Attempts to reassert the authority of the established church after the Restoration met with considerable dissent, and a demand to worship as Bacupians chose, rather than obey some ecclesiastical dictat. In 1690, James Lord of Tunstead and John Hoyle of Bacup each registered their own home as a meeting place for worship.

Then along came two itinerant Yorkshiremen who had heard that lead was cheaper in Bacup than in Cliviger, which was the principal source of lead for Halifax, where they were employed. William Mitchel, a dissenter from Heptonstall, was rapidly becoming known as a formidable preacher. His cousin David Crosley weighed some 20 stones and stood 6 ft 7 ins tall.

In April 1692 a site was purchased for £3 from landowner John Whitaker of Broadclough. The building then erected was to function as a school-house, and a meeting place for Protestant Dissenters, with particular reference to Mitchel and Crosley, being registered for worship on 13 October 1692 as the Mitchel and Crosley Meeting House. Two months earlier, while on a preaching tour of the Midlands, Crosley had been baptised, and thereafter the 'Church of Christ in Rossendale' began to assume predominantly Baptist tenets.

Dr Pococke's two so-called Presbyterian chapels would be the old school-house, which still functioned as a dissenters' place of worship, and the first Ebenezer Baptist society which dated from 1710. There were no other 'chapels' at the time of his visit.

The Methodists arrived during the 1740s. William Darney, a Scotsman akin to John the Baptist and John Knox, preached at Gauxholme (Todmorden) for fourteen successive evenings early in 1745, and among his hearers was a 20-year-old farmworker from Bacup named John Madin (later spelt Maden), who was converted, and subsequently invited Darney to preach at Heap Barn. Here, on Todmorden Old Road at Sharneyford, the first Methodist preaching service in Rossendale took place, and a William Darney society was set up, led by John Madin, who also attended the first-ever Methodist Quarterly Meeting in October 1748 at the Chapel House, Todmorden Edge South, chaired by the evangelical Vicar of Haworth, Rev William Grimshaw.

Methodism grew rapidly, with visits from John Bennet, George Whitefield, and the Wesley brothers, and in 1757 a class meeting was established at Broadclough, which was visited on

20 July 1759 by John Wesley and Rev William Grimshaw, who 'rode to Broad Clough in the afternoon, a lone house in the midst of the Lancashire mountains. The people came in from all quarters, and it was a season of great refreshment'. Grimshaw's involvement stemmed from the inclusion of Bacup in the great Haworth 'Round'.

Darney was an evangelist, not an organiser and, after a visit by John Wesley in May 1747, the erstwhile William Darney societies were placed under the care of Rev William Grimshaw. As it grew, the embryo Bacup society used the old school-house until the first preaching house in Bacup was built in Lanehead Lane, at an annual rent of one half-penny, on a site currently marked by a commemorative plaque, and visited by John Wesley himself on 14 July 1761. Wesley found the new preaching house 'large, but not large enough to contain the congregation', so in May 1786 tenders were sought for the building of a new Wesleyan chapel. At the same time, the Anglicans were building in Church Street and, as the Wesleyan chapel was completed first in 1787, the Anglican clergyman, Rev John Uttley of Goodshaw, was invited to preach there on Sunday mornings at 10.30 am, following the Wesleyan service at 9 am, reciprocating Mr Uttley's permission to John Wesley to preach in his Goodshaw Parish Church way back in August 1748.

John Hirst (1736-1815), converted among the Wesleyan Methodists, became a class leader and a Methodist local preacher in 1764 at the age of 27, but within a year was suspected of Calvinistic tendencies, excluded from the Methodists, and in May 1773 began the longest pastorate in the history of Ebenezer Baptist Church.

A Bacup man was present when the Particular Baptist Society for Propagating the Gospel amongst the Heathen (later the Baptist Missionary Society) was founded at Kettering on 2 October 1792. Though not officially a founding father, Richard Ashworth of Bacup, a traveller in swansdown, happened to be in Kettering at the time. It is on record that the Society began with £13, in the form of promissory notes collected in a snuff-box.

East Lancashire originally belonged to the Diocese of Coventry and Lichfield, but in 1541 the independent Diocese of Chester was formed, whose Bishop William Cleaver came to consecrate Bacup's first Anglican church on 16 August 1788. St John's was originally a chapel-of-ease attached to St Nicholas', Newchurch, but in 1837 the original township of Bacup became for religious purposes 'the Consolidated Chapelry of St John's' — and the church was elevated to the status of 'Bacup Parish Church', familiarly known as 'Th'owd Parish Church', where Justice Whitaker, in true Scriptural fashion, used to go the rounds of the beerhouses and the streets on a late Sunday morning, and compel them to come in . . .

Four years later, Tunstead Church was built in the 'Booth' district, while in 1854 Christ Church (1000 acres) was also carved out of the Parish of St John on land given by Rev James Heyworth of Bristol, one of the Heyworths of Greensnook.

The first united Sunday School procession in Bacup marked the coronation day of George IV on 19 July 1821, when scholars belonging to the Episcopal Church (St John's), Wesleyan (Mount Pleasant) and Baptist (Ebenezer) Sunday Schools were each treated to a spice cake, a glass of beer, and a sixpence after their procession around Bacup.

The rapid growth of industrialisation and the resulting increase in population led to more places of worship. Irwell Terrace seceded from Ebenezer in 1821, the Primitive Methodists arrived in 1824, and the Wesleyan Methodist Association in 1836, building their original 'Shareholders' Chapel' in November 1838, so termed because funds were raised by issuing £1 shares bearing interest at 4½%. The Congregationalists followed in 1848 and, when the Salford Catholic Diocese was formed in 1850, Rev Henry Joseph Mulvaney was sent to darkest Bacup as missionary rector, and St Mary's began in a garret over a shop at 33 Market Street in the suimmer of 1852, building their church on Bankside five years later.

By this time an educational inspector in June 1849 remarked that the prevailing sect was the Particular Baptists and, when the Ecclesiastical Census took place on 30 March 1851, there were three Particular Baptist congregations in Bacup alone, excluding Stacksteads — more than any other denomination. In all, 11,470 Bacup and Stacksteads folk out of a total population of about 14,000 attended worship on Census Sunday, compared with a national proportion of 7,261,032 out of a population of just under 18 million.

Most churches had Sunday Schools, which frequently taught the three Rs. Many children would not have learned to read otherwise. Diligent youngsters at Ebenezer received 1d for reciting poetry, 2d for a hymn, and 3d for a psalm or portion of Scripture. In 1843 figures show 2,901 scholars attending Bacup Sunday Schools, a figure which by 1878 had risen to 6,354, after which a slow but steady decline began, though the Rossendale Sunday School Union, which began on New Year's Day 1844 with six Baptist Sunday Schools, had 18 Bacup Sunday Schools affiliated by 1930 — 598 teachers and 3,819 scholars.

Both Methodists and Baptists were concerned about poorer youngsters, who could not afford 'Sunday clothes'. The Wesleyans initiated the Bacup Ragged School, opened in a room in Union Street, to look after children in the Club Houses area. By 1854 it had 103 scholars, and appeared on the Wesleyan circuit plan for twenty years with a 2½ appointment every Sunday. When it became overcrowded, a new school-chapel was built a mere 250 yards away on Alma Street, but this was enough to deter some of the poorer children from coming, and it soon lost the 'Ragged School' tag.

The Baptist effort came later. The Blue Ribbon was the badge of all total abstainers, and the movement began as a temperance reform club in America in the early 1870s, reaching England in 1877. Campaigns were held in Bacup during the summer of 1882, resulting in 4,500 'soldiers' and the formation of a Blue Ribbon Union whose members paid 1s per quarter and met at the Coffee Tavern in Church Street. Early in 1883 it took the name of the Gospel Temperance Union and on 21 July opened a new 'barracks' at Lower Rockliffe, one of two causes initiated by Ebenezer Baptist Church. The Newgate Mission was established in the centre of a lodging-house population and followed the lines of a 'ragged school'.

Religious influence was strong, most of the mill-owners being godly men who had established such good relations with their workforce that trade unions were considered unnecessary and strikes were an unknown phenomenon for most of the Victorian era. Their word was their bond — jannock.

Employment did not depend on any church or chapel connection but, although the Baptist Church was under no-one's patronage, it was certainly an advantage to be a worshipper at Ebenezer if a job was sought at the Holmes Mill of George Shepherd of Shepherd's Tent (named after his favourite Bible verse — Isaiah 38 v 12) and his brother James. Beatrice Potter felt in 1886 that 'the Churches and non-conformity in particular had such a grip on the town's life that if people did not go to worship at either church or chapel, then they found it difficult to get work'.

Ebenezer even had their own hymnbook, *Sacred Songs for Baptist Schools,* eight of whose 500 hymns were written by their own people, including Thomas Allen, who came from Coventry in November 1875 to begin work as a 'Pedlar for God', under the auspices of the Metropolitan Colportage Association, at an annual salary of £80, which eventually proved insufficient to make family ends meet. During his 5½ years as a colporteur, he sold well over 30,000 items, and concentrated on visiting 'those who attend no place of worship'. He resigned in April 1881 and became a greengrocer.

Bacup Wesleyan Circuit existed as an independent entity for 55 years, and hived off the Rawtenstall section as a separate circuit in 1866. When the number of places in Bacup was assessed on 1 December 1873, there were nine chapels with 5790 sittings, making Bacup the most capacious circuit in the whole Wesleyan connexion in terms of averages. In fact, in 1881, circuit steward Edward Hoyle was contemplating a proposal to further divide the Bacup Circuit, which at the time comprised nine chapels with four ministers and 1,193 members, but was persuaded to forget the idea. In May 1882, Bacup's 1,333 membership was the highest in the whole Bolton & Rochdale District — and the highest ever recorded.

The following year, Wesleyan Methodism's first illustrated weekly newspaper rolled off a Bacup printing press — the evangelical *Joyful News*, printed at the Rossendale Printing Works in Bacup by William John Tyne, and first issued on 22 February 1883. The paper was printed in Bacup for exactly seven years, until it was selling 50,000 copies a week, when Tyne moved to Stockport, where the number of trains per day was considerably more than the 24 which ran from Bacup to Manchester.

The new St John's Church, with its unusual sloping floor from font to chancel, was consecrated by Bishop James Fraser of Manchester on 21 June 1883, replacing the original premises, which had proved structurally inadequate and collapsed in April 1871.

When Queen Victoria celebrated her Golden Jubilee in 1887, Bacup could boast a total of 9,235 Sunday school scholars and teachers and, when a local religious census took place on 29 January 1887, 51% of the Bacup population attended worship — 12,768 out of a population of 25,034. The Salvation Army aggregated the most (1,220), followed by Mount Pleasant Wesleyans (983) and St Mary's Roman Catholics (838), whose morning attendance was the highest at 569.

During 1892, when the number of Catholics in Stacksteads was 769, St Joseph's Mission was formed, building a new school-chapel which was dedicated in December 1897, and used as a worship centre until the church was opened on 19 February 1928.

By the dawning of the 20th century, Rossendale had become the 'Baptist Valley', with ten places of worship in Bacup and Stacksteads. Among them was Mount Olivet, set up by Rev Jonas Smith, a Particular Baptist who pastored Ebenezer until the end of 1874, when he felt impelled to set up his own Gospel Mission in the Co-operative Hall. This became Mount Olivet, known as the Tin Chapel, after the use of an iron building retrieved from Waterfoot in 1894. Mr Smith was so particular about hymns sung there that verses which offended his interpretation of Scripture were blacked out in the hymnbooks . . .

The singing tradition was important. 'Vital Spark' was a regular item at funerals, especially Baptist ones. Most churches had their choirs, and several their bell-ringers. The Strict and Particular Baptist choirs met annually for a Choirs Gathering from 1891 until 1985, paying five visits to Bacup as the guest of Providence, Tong(u)e Meadow, their first in 1897.

Beatrice Potter, visiting Bacup, felt as if she were 'living through a page of puritan history'. In 1890 the Rossendale Society for Visiting and Instructing the Blind was formed. In addition, local sick or benevolent societies helped to provide some security in days when there was no state assistance. All denominations had them, Waterside being the first (1841), followed by St Saviour's (1859) and Acre Mill (1883). Members at Waterside paid 1s per month, which entitled them to sick pay and their relatives to a death grant of £8. Thus the Church attempted to alleviate the sufferings of humanity.

> OPPOSITE: The old St John's Church, built 1787-8, and which collapsed 13 April 1861, by which time over 7,000 interments had taken place in the churchyard. It is shown propped up during 1866. (BNHS) LEFT: Justice Whitaker (1789-1855) — from the painting in Winsley Hall. He was Bacup's first magistrate, a prominent churchman, and owned 577 acres of land in the Bacup area. (WJW) RIGHT: Beatrice Potter, grand-daughter of Lawrence Heyworth of Greensnook, as she appeared on the first of her two visits to Bacup in 1883. She married the socialist Sidney Webb in 1892.

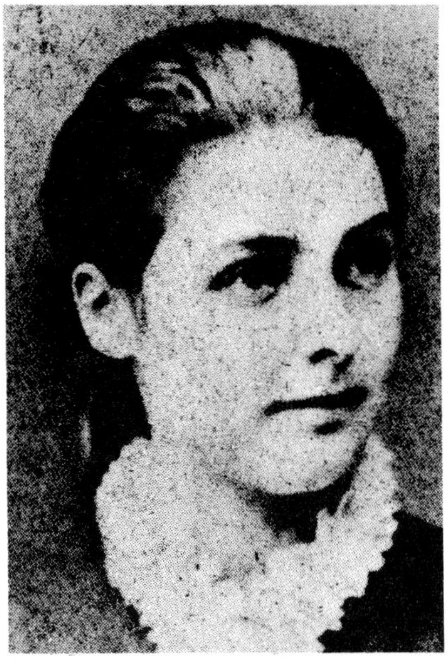

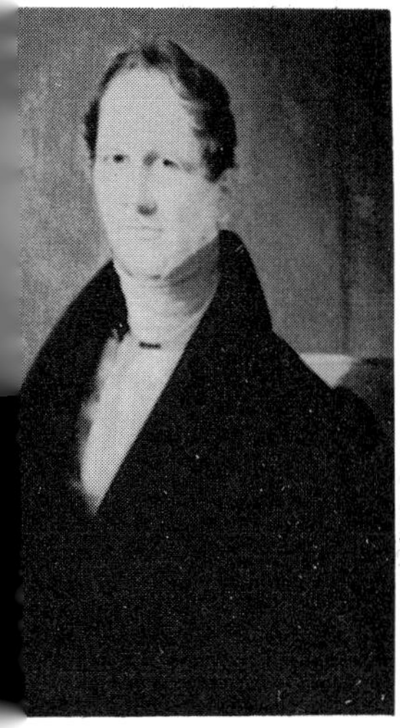

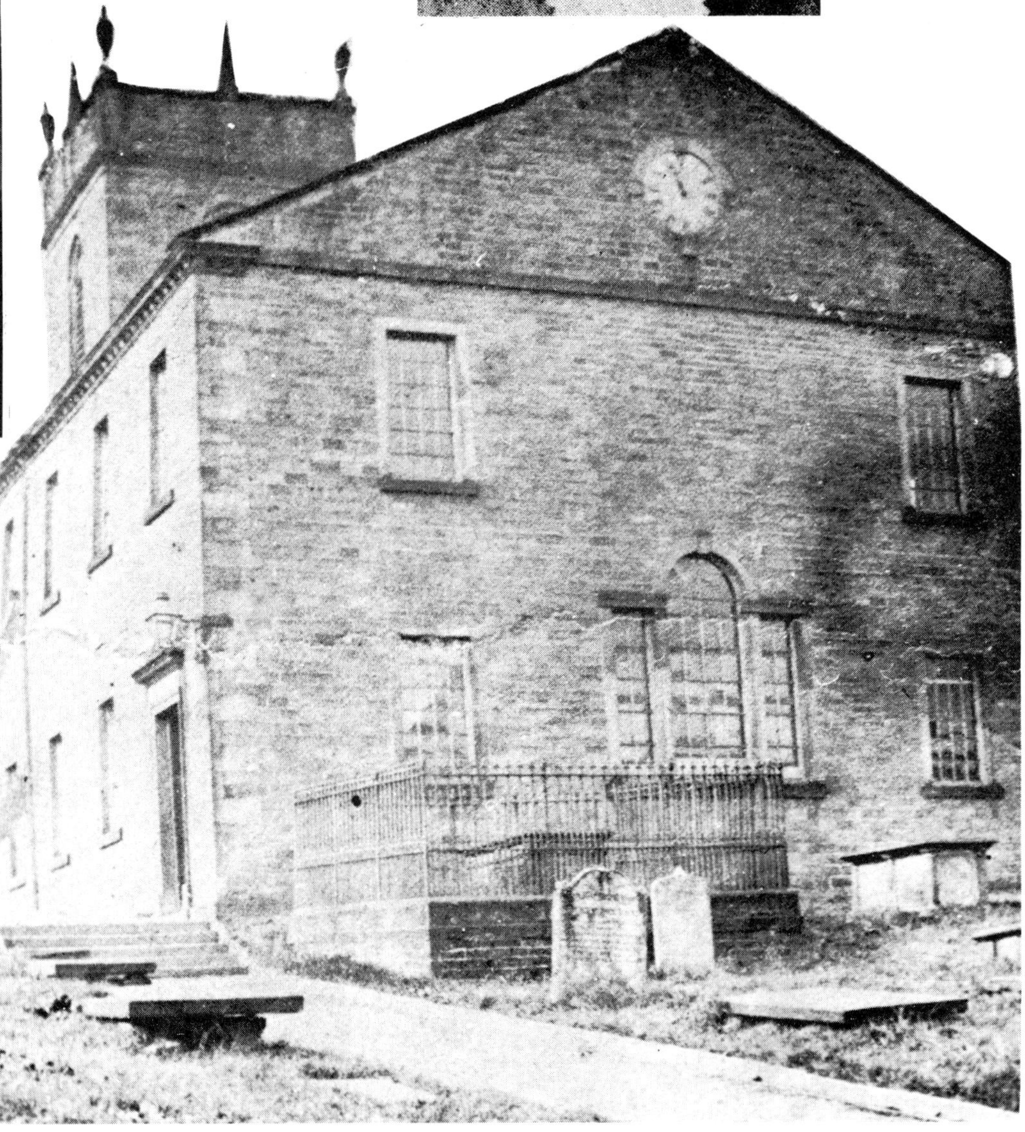

LEFT: Rev John Hirst (1736-1815), Ebenezer Baptist Church's longest-serving pastor. RIGHT: Oak preaching chair used by Hirst and presented by A. J. Cooper in 1909 — the attached plate inscribed with the name of the donor and the date. Carelessly thrown away during refurbishment, the chair was lovingly reconstructed by Alan Stansfield and is safely preserved at Trinity. (AS) BELOW: Ebenezer Baptist Chapel, mother of all Baptist churches in the area. The imposing chapel was built 1868-70, and the adjoining school, remodelled from the 1812 chapel at a cost of £1,100 after the roof was found to be insecure, was used as both school and chapel until 1870. The premises were demolished 1964/65.

ABOVE: St Mary's Catholic Church, built 1857, with the original presbytery behind; this latter was damaged by fire in 1944 when the priest barely escaped. BELOW: Mount Pleasant Wesleyan Chapel, the earliest Methodist cause in Bacup. These premises were built 1840 and demolished 1952/3.

	30 March 1851				29 January 1887			
	Morn.	Aft.	Eve.	Total	Morn.	Aft.	Eve.	Total
BAPTIST:								
Waterbarn	420	460	200	1080	355	384	-	739
Ebenezer	500	750	200	1450	392	-	282	674
Zion					268	-	229	497
Irwell Terrace	800	980	300	2080	235	-	173	408
Doals					152	224	-	376
Acre Mill					197	-	129	326
Providence	41	54	-	95	98	93	-	191
Mount Olivet					114	-	96	210
General Baptist					72	79	-	151
WESLEYAN:								
Mount Pleasant	1053	-	855	1908	532	-	451	983
Wesley Place					278	-	222	500
Stacksteads	172	172	100	444	301	-	194	495
Thorn					202	-	262	464
Heald					-	206	98	304
Britannia					131	-	90	221
Sharneyford					-	75	-	75
ANGLICAN:								
St John's	600	800	-	1400	229	-	387	616
Holy Trinity, Tunstead	325	393	-	718	296	-	275	571
Christ Church					242	-	143	385
St Saviour's					360	-	166	526
PRIMITIVE METHODISTS:								
Bacup	248	350	203	801	155	-	158	313
Stacksteads	41	101	62	204	-	133	91	224
Change					-	52	27	79
Britannia United Methodist					-	204	117	321
Waterside United Methodist	272	353	420	1045	168	-	123	291
St Mary's Roman Catholic					569	269	-	838
Congregationalists	74	100	62	236	134	-	120	254
Blue Ribbon Mission					-	-	103	103
Spiritualists					-	196	217	413
Salvation Army					-	572	648	1220
TOTALS:	4546	4513	2402	11,461	5480	2417	4801	12,768

PROGRAMME.

PARTICULAR Baptist Choirs' 23rd Annual Friendly Gathering.

To be held at
PROVIDENCE
STRICT
BAPTIST
CHAPEL,
TONG, BACUP,

On Saturday
Afternoon,
June 21st, 1913.

Chairman:
Mr. B. W. WARBURTON.
Vice-Chairmen:
Mr. P. HALLIWELL and
Mr. J. CROFT.
Conductor:
Mr. D. HOWORTH.
Organist:
Mr. J. H. LORD.

Not only Singers
but all friends are
cordially invited.

TEA will be provided for which a charge of 1/- each will be made.   Tea on the Tables at 4 o'clock prompt.

W. MADEN, 10, Crooked Shore, Bacup,
J. R. NEWELL, 7, Albert Terrace, Bacup, } *Hon. Secretaries.*

John Heywood Ltd., Music Printers, Manchester and London.

LEFT: Thomas Allen (1849-1901), colporteur who sold Bibles and other literature under the auspices of the Metropolitan Colportage Association 1877-1881. RIGHT: Church attendances, as recorded in the censuses of March 1851 and January 1887. BELOW: Cover of programme for the 23rd Annual Friendly Gathering of the Strict and Particular Baptist Choirs. They paid five visits to Bacup, the first in 1897, and met annually for 95 years from 1891 until 1985.

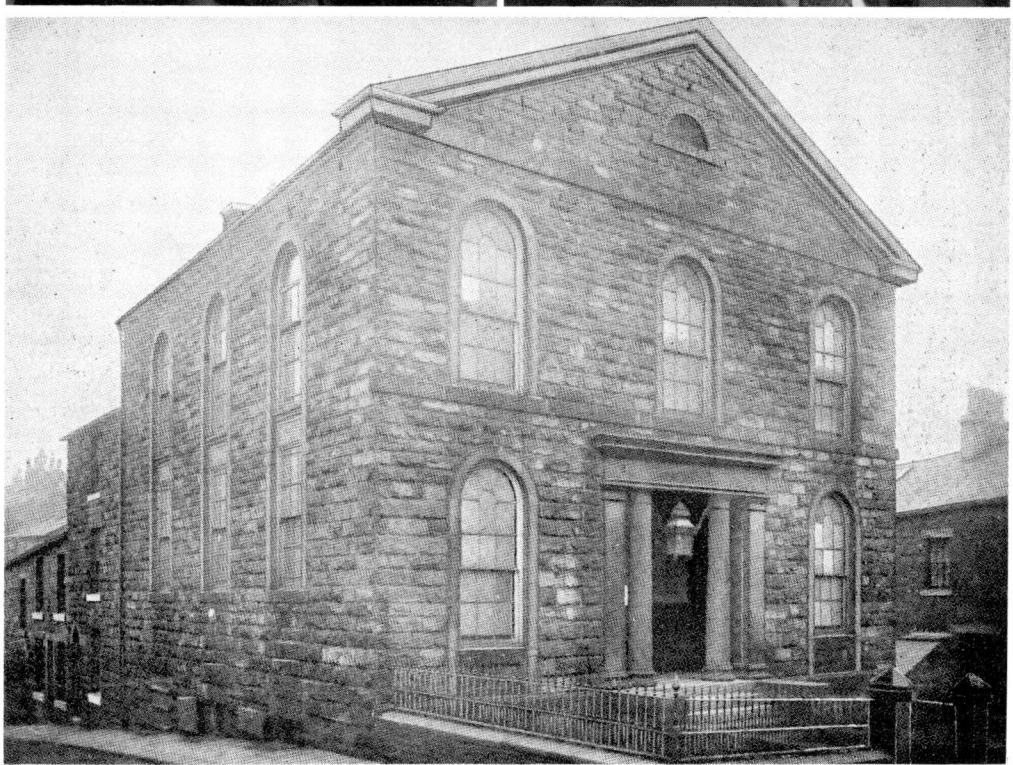

Stalwarts of the Rossendale Society for Visiting and Instructing the Blind: ABOVE: Lot Crook (1865-1938), teacher and visitor for the Society for 36 years (1891-1927), appointed at a salary of £1 per week. He also repaired boots and shoes, re-seated chairs, tuned pianos, was a teacher and class leader at Thorn Wesleyan chapel, and in demand as a singer, despite being blind from birth. RIGHT: Frank Haworth (1901-1976), secretary of the Society for 38 years, was Bacup's original 'angry young man', detested hypocrisy in all its forms, and was outspoken on behalf of the underprivileged, becoming a local and county councillor, and Freeman of Bacup in 1959. (WMH) BELOW: North Street Primitive Methodist Church, built in Brickfield 1853-4 on land owned by mill-owner Robert Smith. Smith Brow, which led up to the front entrance, ran between the present Bacup Health Centre and Tong Mill, and did not feature on the 1851 map (see endpaper). Capable of seating 600, it closed at the end of 1941 and was demolished in summer 1952.

ABOVE: Todmorden Penny Post — addressed to John Holt of Stubbylee, 31 January 1840 — one of the earliest examples of Penny Post. (RC) (I) below: Horse-drawn 'bus operated by W. Roberts & Company Ltd outside Edwin Birch's Spread Eagle Inn at Rochdale. It ran six services a day between Bacup and Rochdale by 1867. (BNHS)

On the Right Tracks

In mediaeval days, ancient tracks were followed, usually at night, by pack horses or 'lime-gals' (galloway ponies) bearing their burdens of lime or salt. The last of the lime-gal drivers was Mary Alice Hartley, better known as Ailse o'Fusser's, who died in February 1880. The Pennine boundary became known as Limers' Gate, an ancient highway linking Rochdale and Clitheroe. This roughly followed the eastern Bacup boundary from Trough Gate at Britannia, above Sharneyford and Heald, and over Deerplay to Windy Bank and Crown Point. This became a turnpike road in 1755 and at Deerplay Bar met another old road traversing Rooley Moor and the Lumb Valley.

Two ancient trackways from Britannia converged beyond Causeway House, and reached the centre of Bacup *via* Tong Lane, one of two main roads faced by the George & Dragon Inn, the other being Lane Head Lane which linked with the old road to Sharneyford. Rochdale Road did not exist.

Road maintenance, if any, stemmed from an Act of 1555 making the inhabitants of a parish responsible for the upkeep of highways through their area — most of which were simply rights of way across country, and little more than well-used packhorse tracks, old highways and narrow bridle paths.

After 1755, turnpike trusts enabled gates or bars to be erected across specific stretches of road, and tolls to be levied for improvement and maintenance. (The gates were named turnpikes from their resemblance to a barrier of pikes or bars sharpened at one end and attached at the other to a rotating upright pole or axle).

The Haslingden and Todmorden Turnpike of 1789 followed the line of the present Booth Road (familiarly known throughout the 19th century as the Old Road) through to Bacup and over Lanehead and Todmorden Old Road to that town, which was until 1888 wholly in Lancashire. This superseded a packhorse road *via* Oakenhead Wood and Tunstead Lane.

Bacup eventually had a total of eleven toll bars — at Tunstead, Stacksteads, Height Barn, Britannia, Swan Bar, Rockliffe (Sheephouse), Sharneyford, Deerplay, Broadclough, Underbank, and Tong — where the owners of the nearby Bacup Corn Mill had two rights of way, one above and one below the toll post, exempting the millowners from toll charges at that specific point. Turnpike roads, developed for the use of horse-drawn coaches, were supposed to be well surfaced, but William Lee in 1849 had his reservations, and recommended the use of gas tar, mixed with ashes and gravel taken out of the river bed laid at a cost of 1s per square yard. Tolls were meant to pay for road building and repair and, in 1796 for example, the toll bar at Four Lane Ends took £173 and Sharneyford £166. Four years later, receipts at Sharneyford Toll Bar were £283, and at Four Lane Ends £261. In 1875 receipts from the four bars active in the Bacup Local Board district were said to average £65 a week.

The road from Rawtenstall to Waterfoot was constructed in 1826 under the supervision of John Loudon MacAdam (who gave his name to the macadamising of present road surfaces), and two years later was extended through the Thrutch to Bacup. The Thrutch Gorge is over half a mile long, 120 feet deep, and barely wide enough to accommodate both the River Irwell and the main road from Waterfoot to Bacup, to say nothing of the railway which followed a quarter of a century later.

By now there was a postal service, of sorts, a messenger on horseback leaving Bacup Fold at 8 am for Rochdale four days a week; his journey took three hours each way. A similar service operated from Newchurch to Rochdale *via* Rooley Moor. During March and April 1803, Bacup letters averaged 96 per week, at 2d each — double the charge for the rest of Rossendale. By 1824 Bacup was served by the Rochdale Penny Post, arriving at 9 am, and Newchurch half an hour later. The Todmorden Penny Post also served Bacup — *via* Rochdale.

The earliest Post Office in Bacup is shown in St James Street in 1845, when letters arrived from Rochdale at 10.30 am, being despatched to Rochdale at 3 pm. Bacup's first 'letter' carrier was paid a penny for every letter delivered, the accumulation of which was reckoned as his wages.

Horse-drawn coaches provided the earliest public transport, and remained in vogue until the early 20th century. The best-known local company was founded by William Roberts in 1864 as the Bacup Omnibus Conveyance and Livery Stables Co. It operated four through services a day to Rochdale from the George & Dragon Inn (where stabling existed for 14 horses). Journey time was an hour and five minutes. The reverse trip took fifteen minutes longer. The company also ran horse-buses to Burnley *via* Water every Monday at 9.30 am, and to Rawtenstall and Haslingden.

At its peak, the Rossendale Division Carriage Company (as it became known) owned nearly 100 horses, and specialised in weddings (for which it had six specially-groomed white horses with reins covered in white silk, and flowers decorating the coach), funeral parties, and picnic outings. When the steam trams arrived in 1889, almost 40 horses, plus three omnibuses and three waggonettes owned by the Company, were sold at auction.

Steam trams made their appearance on 3 August 1889 — a steam engine and usually one carriage. The original idea was for trams from Rawtenstall to terminate in Bacup at the bottom of Church Street, but the manoeuvre into the turning triangle at 'Burton's corner' proved too dangerous, so the terminus was fixed outside the new Market Hotel. The construction of the tramways included paving with stone setts and their upkeep between the tramlines and eighteen inches on either side, so that when Bacup Corporation applied for funds to pave Burnley Road, Rochdale Road, and Yorkshire Street in September 1912, they were basically completing a job already begun.

When news was received at 3 pm on 6 May 1897 of a fire at Warth Mill, Waterfoot, engineer John H. Jackson with three firemen and driver Ingram turned out with the steam fire engine (the *Irwell*), quickly followed by Captain John Harland (Chief Constable) on his bicycle, while the rest of the fire crew travelled by tram. They reached the scene at 3.20 pm.

After 20 years, the steam trams, known as the Baltic Fleet, were replaced by the electric variety, the first two steered from the Thrutch to Bacup by the Mayoress and Deputy Mayoress of Bacup. Two years later almost to the day (Tuesday, 25 July 1911), Rochdale Corporation extended their tramway operations to Bacup, terminating in Bridge Street. Trams ran to both Rochdale and Rawtenstall every 15 minutes, and every ten minutes on Wednesday and Saturday afternoons.

A through tram route from Rochdale to Rawtenstall was agreed in principle, but would have been impossible because the line from Bacup to Rawtenstall was narrower than the one to Rochdale. Bacup, which municipally had no say in either, was the only point of connection (though not literally) between the four-foot gauge tramways of North Lancashire and the 4ft 8½ inches lines of South Lancashire.

Meanwhile, the Whitworth Vale Motor Bus Company ran a Pioneer service spasmodically between Healey and Bacup around 1907, as did Rossendale Division Carriage Company in 1909. The latter also operated services to Britannia and Weir — the latter hitherto neglected as far as public transport was concerned. After the Great War Allen's Motors (Bacup) operated omnibus services to Deerplay and Sharneyford, using a Daimler omnibus purchased from the War Disposals Board at Slough. These services did not prove successful, however, and were soon withdrawn. (At the end of 1923, Todmorden Corporation initiated a 'bus service to Burnley *via* Bacup).

Soon afterwards the Allen brothers (sons of Ebenezer colporteur Thomas Allen) sold their interest in the family business, and Herbert Allen secured employment with Holt Bros (Rochdale) Ltd — the Yellow Coaches — as General Manager. This was in 1926.

The Bacup to Accrington semi-express service began on 14 January 1929, initially on an hourly frequency, later becoming half-hourly. The Waterfoot to Britannia service *via* Booth Road and New Line began on 1 June 1930, while after Easter 1931 traffic lights appeared in the town centre. A year later 'buses took over from trams on the Rawtenstall to Bacup route, by which time Holt Bros had gone into liquidation, and Herbert Allen had become managing director of Yelloway Motor Services Ltd, which ran several daily services through Bacup to Blackpool as well as to London. As late as May 1966 a return ticket from Bacup to London on a Yelloway express cost a mere 42s.

In October 1927 an express 'bus service began from Rochdale to Manchester, extended to Bacup in March 1928, and to Flixton (Jubilee Tree) in May, a total distance of 27.025 miles and a route shared by three operators. The service was eventually cut back to Cannon Street, Manchester, a move bitterly resented by the passengers. In mid-May 1932 'buses replaced trams on the Rochdale-Bacup route, while the Manchester express route was divided in Rochdale. The express journeys on the Manchester side were absorbed into the local no 17 route, and the Bacup section was down-graded to route no 16, a number retained until 'bus services were reorganised in the 1970s. Since 'bus deregulation in 1986, the Bacup-Manchester express 'bus service has been reinstated at peak weekday periods as route no 16.

Plans were afoot for a railway to Bacup in July 1846 from both Bury and Rochdale. The latter was surveyed and staked out, but not completed for another 25 years, though the line to Rawtenstall opened on 28 September 1846, and the extension to Newchurch (Waterfoot) on 27 March 1848. Travellers from Bacup were catered for by horse-drawn coaches which three mornings a week connected with a 9 am express train from Rawtenstall to Salford.

The first passenger train ran from Bacup to Manchester on 1 October 1852, when the first train out in the morning was the Parliamentary or Government Class train, to conform to a directive that all railways must run at least one train over all lines on their systems at a fare of not more than one penny per mile. In the timetables these trains were designated by 'Parl' or 'Gov'. Fares from Bacup to Manchester in 1854 were 4s first-class, 3s 2nd-class, and 1s 10d 3rd-class. In 1876 the railway company decided to paint all their first-class carriages yellow, second-class brown, and third-class blue, with tickets in corresponding colours, so that passengers had a good visible guide to their respective carriages. Second-class was eventually abolished in 1912, and third-class officially upgraded to 2nd-class in 1956.

Originally, the whole of the line from Stubbins to Bacup was single-track, but the volume of traffic made it necessary to double the track between Stubbins and Rawtenstall, which was done by July 1857. In November 1870 another line opened, from Rochdale to Facit. Plans were passed for an extension to Bacup in 1872, but nearly six years passed before any positive action was taken. It was supposed to be completed by August 1879, but in the event took a full two years longer, the cost more than doubling by the time it was finished. To compensate for the delay, a double line would be constructed from Newchurch to Bacup. This necessitated the construction of a 592-yards long Newchurch no 3 tunnel through solid rock, which the navvies dubbed 'The Thrutch', and which officialdom ratified. ('Thrutch' is an expressive Lancashire dialect word akin to 'striving and straining to the limit of one's endurance'.) It also proved necessary to widen the neighbouring tunnels and to rebuild both Bacup and Stacksteads stations (reopened 23 July 1880), and the widened line was eventually opened on 17 March 1881.

Eventually, at 7.15 am on Thursday, 1 December 1881, the first through train for Rochdale left Bacup with 58 passengers. Just beyond Britannia it reached the highest point on the Lancashire and Yorkshire railway — 967 feet above sea-level at Trough Gate. Trains took 31 minutes to climb up from Rochdale to Bacup, but despite the initial 1 in 34 climb out of Bacup, did the return trip in 26 minutes. The return fare to Rochdale at the time was half a crown. However, Rossendale manufacturers found it cheaper and quicker to send cotton pieces to Manchester by road rather than by rail, for the speed of trains between Bacup and Facit was restricted to 10 mph.

Bacup was meant to be on a through line linking Colne, Burnley, Bacup, Rochdale, Heywood and Manchester. Nothing ever came of that, nor of a Manchester-Newcastle-Glasgow line, projected in 1892, and which envisaged a new Bacup station perhaps in the vicinity of Stubbylee, where a small platform already served the private residents of Stubbylee Hall and Rockcliffe House.

The quarries were served by railways before public transport arrived on the scene, the first railway system in Stacksteads serving Siddall's quarries. Goods traffic was worked mainly from Bacup westwards. In the hey-day of the quarries at Britannia, three goods trains a day left Britannia Sidings (closed 1944), all going *via* Whitworth to Rochdale. The gradient from Britannia station to Bacup was considered too steep for heavy goods trains. It was by this means that stone from Brandwood Quarry was conveyed to London and used as paving stones in Trafalgar Square in 1924.

The Rochdale passenger line closed as an economy measure during the fuel crisis of 1947, but never re-opened to passenger traffic after 14 June 1947, when the last Rochdale train pulled out of Bacup station at 7.55 pm — though goods traffic continued until the railway closed completely on 21 August 1967.

The introduction of diesels in February 1956 resulted in a temporary boost to passenger traffic on the remaining line which more than doubled the figures for the previous year, and the journey time of 16½ minutes to Bury revived memories of the apocryphal *Stacksteads Flyer* of many years earlier, being nicknamed the *Tally-Ho*. But eventually Dr Richard Beeching's proposals meant the end of the line for Bacup railway traffic, and the last scheduled passenger train left Bacup on Saturday, 3 December 1966. The long Thrutch tunnel is now blocked up, and one of the others is part of the Irwell Valley pedestrian walkway.

Since the end of the railways, Bacup has been served by 'buses which provide a direct link with neighbouring towns and the Fylde coast. It is no longer obliged to live in splendid isolation.

ABOVE: The Whitworth Vale Motor Omnibus Company Ltd's *The Pioneer*, linking Rochdale and Bacup, 1907. BELOW: *The Irwell* — Bacup's first fire engine, horse-drawn, 1893-1916, shown with crew. (HO'N)

ABOVE: Opening of the Bacup to Rochdale tramway, 25 July 1911; the line from Shawforth to Bacup was opened at noon, providing a through service to Rochdale for the first time. BELOW: Reputedly the last steam car in England, at the entrance to Fern Hill estate, 20 July 1909; a postcard of this picture records: 'Through storm and shine, I've run my race, Electric cars now take my place; For twenty years you've heard my bell, But best of friends must say "farewell!". (BNHS)

ABOVE: Day out from Ross Mill, 1924 — Bacup Motor Garage of South Street provided the vehicle, which was limited to 12 mph. William Rigby, photographer, of Southport, took this picture as the vehicle arrived — the ninth coach that day, with copies available by the end of the afternoon. BELOW: Bacup engine shed was L&YR shed no 21, and in 1948 had 37 locomotives allocated. It closed 10 October 1954 when only eight were left.

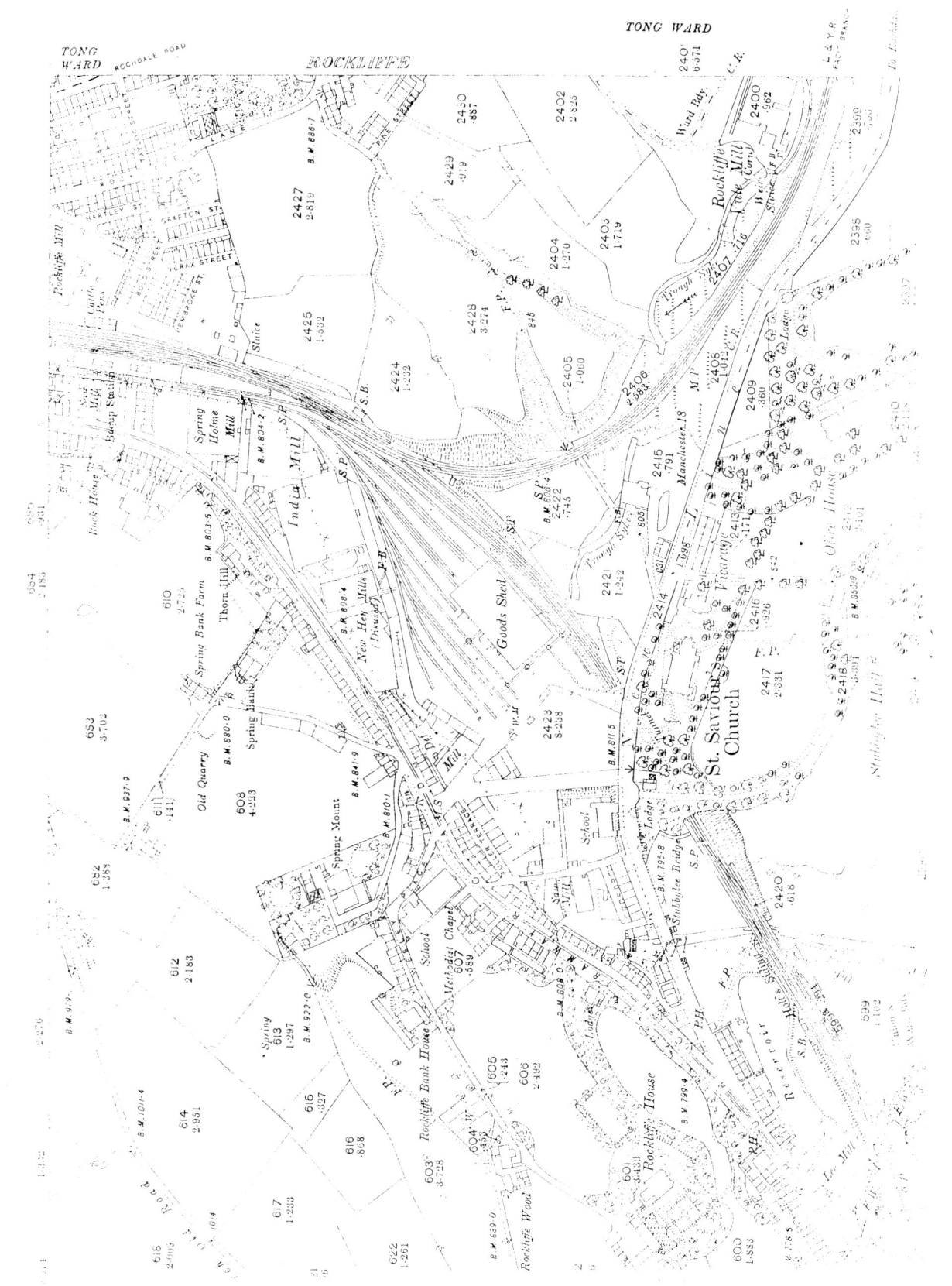

The 1891 Ordnance Survey map shows the railway lines from Bacup station to Holt's Siding, and on the Facit branch towards Rochdale. Ross Mill was not yet built.

Threads of Industry

The parish registers of Newchurch between 1705 and 1707 record some 23 woollen workers in the Bacup area. Woollen weaving began as a domestic cottage industry in hillside farms, and during the 18th century progressed from home to factory as out-put proved insufficient to meet growing demand. The seven principal merchants of Bacup in 1787 were all woollen manufacturers, including John Lord of Greensnook, who in the Poor Law assessments of 1745 was assessed 5s for a mill, probably Honey Hole (later Spring Gardens), the only mill in Bacup at that time. In 1751 he was still assessed at 5s, but by 1757 his assessment had risen to £1.

As demand for yarn outstripped supply, John Maden (1724-1809) adapted the fly-shuttle produced in 1733 by John Kay. To the great-great-great-grandfather of Sir John Henry Maden is attributed the application of wheels to the old bocking shuttles on the handlooms, a device which made them run more smoothly, and enabled a single weaver to manage the loom. Bockings, a type of coarse woollen cloth, were named after the town in Essex whence the trade originated.

Until the advent of the Industrial Revolution, the handloom was the mainstay of life. The 'heirloom' originated as the family loom passed from generation to generation; while the 'spinster' (originally denoting her former employment) derives from the custom of an unmarried woman spinning yarn to weave her household linen before marriage. Cotton spinning was also done by hand on a spinning wheel in many hillside cottages and farms.

The first cotton 'factory' in Rossendale was established in 1770 when a few handlooms for the weaving of muslins were set up in a small workshop at the corner of Lanehead Lane, operated on cottage industry lines. Contributory factors included James Hargreaves' spinning jenny (1764/6), Richard Arkwright's spinning frame (1769), and Samuel Crompton's mule (1779), all invented by Lancastrians, plus Edmund Cartwright's power loom (1785).

The geographical conditions of the Lancashire Pennines were ideal for the embryo cotton industry. Bacup water was clean, soft, and free from lime, and its ample supply resulted in the rapid growth of cotton manufacture. Bacup's climate was also damp, with an annual rainfall averaging 50.87 inches over 58 years, and humid — enabling the cotton thread to be spun more easily.

Bacup's first cotton mill was built in 1799 in Church Street (which ran from St John's Church to the town centre). In 1836 it was leased to James Aitken for 31 years, and two years later his son Thomas built a new mill at Underbank, running the business with his brother after the death of their father in February 1841.

James Aitken, along with Robert Munn, provided employment for many families from East Anglia under the migration scheme of 1835, which aimed to meet the demand for labour in the northern textile districts. One Suffolk family was offered wages in Bacup amounting to 29s 6d per week in the first year, rising to 42s a week in the third year. They travelled to London and the north (wearing flannel undergarments, recommended as 'conducive to health') by canal boat, at a fare of 14s per adult and 2s for each of five children under 14. Baby George travelled free. Four months later, John Brett expressed his gratitude for better food, regular wages, and regular work — at Aitken's Church Street mill, where his children were working the standard working week of 69 hours (12 per day plus 9 hours on Saturday), and the overlookers never beat them. A 14-hour working day was commonplace. Adult cotton spinners regularly worked from 6 am to 8 pm (4 pm on Saturdays), a working week of 80 hours and, because of the heat and slippery floors, women generally worked barefoot.

More labour was imported from Ireland. The Irish came to work in the fields, the factories, the mines and quarries. By the time of the 1841 Census, more than one third of the total Irish in England lived in Lancashire, and a further exodus due to the Irish potato famine gave Lancashire a total of 191,506 Irish-born residents in 1851.

The increase in population and the beginnings of the industrial age brought an increase in crime. Some, such as counterfeiting money by clipping Spanish pieces of eight and Portuguese pesetas to make fake golden guineas and sovereigns, was due to the underlying poverty of the working class. Among these forgers were three Bacup men — inn-keeper William Roberts of the George & Dragon, previously 'a man of good character', Israel Wilde of Deerplay, and a man named Turner, who was later hanged.

Four Whitworth men were hanged in November 1809 for uttering forged Bank of England notes. The poverty and resentment of the working class was made worse by the 'sixpenny down' race, when manufacturers, under pressure because of reduced profit margins, passed that reduction on to the weaver in the form of sixpence less on each succeeding piece.

Longer hours and lower wages persisted into the spring of 1826, when the Lancashire weavers' loom-breaking riots, described as 'probably the most dramatic events in the history of the English cotton industry' took place. On 26 April, worried weavers, having smashed power-looms elsewhere in East Lancashire, wreaked havoc in four Bacup mills, destroying 50 looms at Waterbarn, 28 at Tunstead Mill, 28 at Irwell Mill and 52 at Old Clough — a totl of 158 looms, in a massive display of resentment. At the time parish relief for the unemployed varied from 9d to 1s 3d per week. Between the beginning of May and Christmas 1826, the London Relief Committee disbursed almost £27,000 in cash and goods throughout East Lancashire — £700 in Bacup.

On the surface, the 1826 riots were pointless, as the new power-looms (each of which could be operated by one person and could do the work of six handloom weavers) were here to stay. But the riots did help to force the pace of social and factory reform.

When the 1819 Cotton Mills Act forbade the employment of children under the age of nine, many children sought the next best thing, the premises of the dandy loom shops. The dandy loom was one partly adapted with power to draw on the cloth instead of it having to be manually pulled forward by the weaver. At the foot of Maden Road was Park Row, three stone 18th-century houses occupied by weavers who carried on their occupation on the top floors. The middle cottage subsequently became a dandy shop for selling cotton goods, and the row was familiarly known as Dandy Row.

In 1830, Richard Oastler, the 'Factory King', called for a 10-hour day for factory children, supported by 'Honest' John Fielden of Todmorden, whose Bill limited a working week to 60 hours, with 58 the maximum for women and youngsters under 18, but was bitterly opposed by Robert Munn, who never became reconciled to the loss of 'two golden hours' of the working day. And yet Munn employed more Suffolk migrants than anyone else.

Chartism was never strong in Bacup, a mere 15 members being recorded in 1843, but their principles led to the rise of the Co-operative movement, seen as a means of elevating the working class. This began in Bacup when 14 individuals met in the 'Chartists' Room' in Rochdale Road in June 1847, and subscribed sixpence each as the initial capital. By the end of 1856 the Society numbered 1,200 members and had a share capital of £14,700, and eventually new larger premises were opened on Good Friday 1863, followed by seven branches in fairly rapid succession. 15 years later they built three streets on land at Thorn which are still known as the Co-houses. By the time of the Society's Jubilee in 1897, the share capital was £60,000, and on average members spent £46 15s 7¾d each per year.

In its heyday it was possible to obtain almost anything at the Co-op — but not credit. The Co-operative movement encouraged the accumulation of working-class savings through the acquisition of shares and the division of profits among the shareholding members according to the amount of their purchases. By refusing to offer credit, it also encouraged planned budgeting, thrift and frugality.

Performing a similar function was the Bacup Conservative Co-operative Industrial Society Ltd, known as the 'Blue Co', formed after the 1868 General Election, and with a total of 969 members and three branches at its peak in 1884.

In 1865 Bacup had 18 large co-operative cotton mills, the largest being the New Bacup and Wardle Commercial Company, the working man's mill, whose directors were all working men. In 1859 and 1860 it astonished the cotton industry by paying successive half-yearly dividends of 31%, 44% and 62% — this last an achievement no other company could match. They also introduced an American whistle to their Farholme Mill, nicknamed the Yankee Devil, which could be heard four miles away and was the subject of many complaints. Other early and successful industrial co-operatives included the 'Old Co' (Rossendale Industrial Company, who owned Irwell and Weir Mills) and Spring Gardens Cotton Manufacturing Company (1863-1885).

The cotton industry became the staple trade of Bacup for the best part of a century, making Bacup the Valley's first boom town. In 1830 there were 23 mills, in 1881 67, though only 36 a decade later, when 350,000 spindles and 110,000 looms were operating.

As a teenager, Robert Munn worked a 16-hour day and, in 1824 with his brother John, founded a commission house in Manchester, where Robert frequently galloped every morning before breakfast. In the 1830s he built Heath Hill House and Stacksteads Mill, and provided a private fire engine, the *Prince Albert*. Yet Robert Munn petitioned against the application of the 1848 Public Health Act to Bacup, and in 1876 it was reported that he owned six houses in Stacksteads — with not a single privy between them.

Robert Munn died on 19 April 1879 and, when his son Robert Whittaker Munn went out of business locally in 1885, he concentrated his activities on his Manchester business; he died in 1890. His widow left for Scarborough, and soon afterwards his bachelor son Captain Robert Angus Law Munn (1875-1923) also left the area.

Joshua Hoyle (1796-1859) was one of a quartet who set up in business in 1834 at Midge Hole Mill to manufacture calico. After the dissolution of his partnership, he built Plantation Mill in 1841, and later leased Sharneyford and New Hey Mills. By 1851 he employed 271 people. After his death his sons built India Mill (1862), bought Beech Mill (1868), and built Brooksbottom Mill at Summerseat near Bury in 1872, at which time their assets were calculated at about £200,000. Soon afterwards the workers were invited to buy shares in Hoyles' mills at £7 10s each — and did so. By 1921 Hoyles owned nine mills and six subsidiary companies, with total assets of £5,078,655 7s 1d. Twenty years later they controlled 16 factories with an aggregate of 800,000 spindles, 9,740 looms, and 5,600 employees, and in 1943 opened canteens at India and Plantation Mills, charging 9d for meat and veg; 3d for sweet; 2d for soup and 1d for tea. In 1959, seven of the group's mills outside Bacup closed, and at the end of 1963, India and Plantation Mills also closed, followed in March 1981 by Ross Mill, which was not originally part of the group, but acquired by them in December 1920.

The American Civil War resulted in a cotton famine. The supply of cotton to Lancashire fell from its usual 1,116 million lbs in 1860 to an average of 11 million lbs a year in 1862-4, and for nearly three years many people had no work and therefore no income. Soup kitchens opened on a large scale in Bacup and Stacksteads and hundreds of families received poor relief — at their peak 2,500 were in receipt of parish relief, which varied from a quarter to a third of a person's normal earnings, so that a married couple with five children might receive anything from 7s 6d minimum to 17s 6d maximum.

One of the few mills which never stopped running was Holmes Mill, where each worker had one loom, being paid just a bit more than parish relief. This link between the mill-owners, especially the nonconformist ones, and their workers, enabled Bacup to endure the worst effects of the cotton famine without a total breakdown in the social fabric. When the first load of cotton reached Bacup after the end of the American Civil War, workers of both sexes wept for joy and knelt in the streets to thank God.

The cotton famine was the first in a series of damaging setbacks to the cotton trade, though by 1878 the number of spindles in Bacup's mills was at its peak of 520,000 (13,500 looms), but another trade depression lasted twenty years, and caused several mills to close, including Stacksteads, Spring Gardens, and Underbank — which became Rossendale Printing Company's works.

In 1901, the working week was reduced to 55½ hours with a noon finish on Saturdays. At the time there were 5,900 cotton operatives employed in Bacup — 26.43% of the local workforce. A 12-year-old cotton weaver working half-time at Lee Mill worked mornings one week and afternoons the other for half-a-crown a week. When she went to work full-time she earned 5s 6d per week and thought she was well off. By contrast, a teenage weaver at India Mill earned 13s per week.

Other local industries gave their names to Bacup streets — Foundry Street, Forge Street, Brick Street, Coal Pit Lane, and Quarry Street.

Quarrying was a long-standing local industry, at its peak employing 3,000 men. Lee Quarries, the largest in Bacup, initially exported stone on sledges drawn by horses over Rooley Moor to Rochdale, until narrow-gauge railways made transport easier. By 1844 there were 43 small quarries supplying stone for the flagged floors of local mills, roads, dry-stone walls, and other buildings. In cold winter weather, men could be laid off for weeks at a time, and were not paid if they could not work. Frost Holes was aptly named. Local quarrymen, or 'brownbacks', could reputedly out-swear, out-drink and out-eat any competition.

Richard Siddall employed 300 men at his quarries at Lee, Law Head, and Greens Moor at Stacksteads. In 1915 the combined tonnage from Rakehead and Stacksteads quarries was about 1,000 tons a day, or 240,000 tons a year, while in 1928 Henry Heys of Britannia Quarries registered an output of 100,000 tons of stone products a year, some of which was used for the then new East Lancashire road from Salford to Liverpool. Stone from Brandwood Quarries was used to construct the Edenfield bypass and M66, opened in June 1978.

Coal mining in Bacup dates from at least 1631. Most mines were drift mines, and worked a 15-inch seam, the sandrock mine, but tonnages were not high. Old Meadows, opened 1860 and the only local pit with running water in the miners' quarters, produced about 14,000 tons a year. The familiar three-span lattice bridge over Burnley Road carried coal from a new drift mine near Whitaker Clough to the grading machine and coal-loading site of Old Meadows Colliery. The bridge became known as 'th' Owler's bridge' — owler being associated with the alder tree, from which clog soles were made, and used metaphorically as a synonym for clogs. In March 1966 Old Meadows won an award for being the safest pit in the country for its size — but three years later it closed. In practice, heavy snow made it impossible to get to work on the appointed day, so the crucial date was Thursday, 13 March 1969.

The first recorded use of a telephone locally occurred in March 1881, when the home of James Smith Sutcliffe at Beech House was linked to the family Corn Mill some 350 yards away. Three years later, in August 1884, Mr Sutcliffe pioneered the use of electricity, illuminating the Corn Mill with 26 incandescent lamps powered by a self-regulating dynamo.

Rossendale was nothing if not a Valley of Enterprise. In the 1870s the Troy Silver Mining Company promised a new Eldorado in the depths of the United State of Nevada, while J. R. Pilling obtained a concession from the Turkish government in 1890 to build what would have been the longest railway in the world — but both these ventures fell through.

More profitable was the manufacture of footwear. One Suffolk teenager came to Bacup in the 1850s and subsequently opened a shop of his own at 21 Market Street under the sign of the Rossendale Boot & Shoe Exchange. Samuel McLerie is, however, credited with the introduction of the industry to Bacup. In July 1898 he turned the disused Grove cotton mill into Bacup's first footwear factory. In effect he fathered most of the Bacup shoe factories, including J(ack) and J(ames) McLerie's, and the company which in March 1914 became Maden & Ireland, operating from Waterside Mill, and which in 1919 acquired Olive and Kilnholme Mills, and amalgamated with the Rawtenstall Shoe & Slipper Company Ltd.

The Lancashire cotton industry effectively peaked in 1914, when Bacup had 25 textile firms working 9,749 looms and 340,452 spindles, since when a virtually continuous decline set in and, after the Great War, other industries began to take their place. Although threequarters of the felt produced in Britain was made in Rossendale in 1920, none had been produced in Bacup until Lee Mill, denuded of its cotton operatives by national service during the Great War, was taken over by Thomas Gaskell and his sons for felt-making and carpet underlay.

Bacup was proving its versatility in the face of current problems.

LEFT: Joshua Hoyle (1796-1859), Bacup's early 'cotton lord', and his RIGHT: trade device, designed in 1865 by his son Isaac. It consisted of three flags and a ribbon with the words 'Union is Strength'. The idea was to show that American cotton, depicted by the American flag, joined to British labour, produced an article that could not be bettered.

Bacup's BIG THREE in Textiles

for Spinning and Weaving

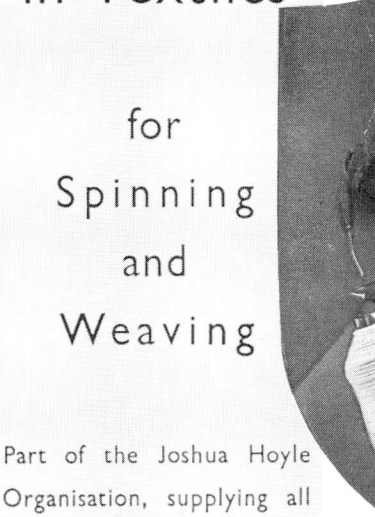

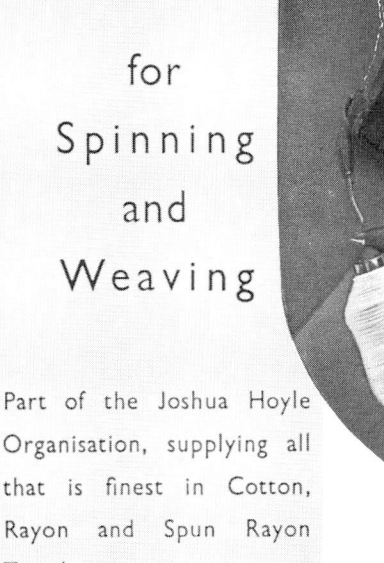

INDIA MILL

ROSS MILL

PLANTATION MILL

Part of the Joshua Hoyle Organisation, supplying all that is finest in Cotton, Rayon and Spun Rayon Textiles.

Joshua Hoyle AND SONS (BACUP) LTD

INDIA MILL . ROSS MILL . PLANTATION MILL . BACUP

Joshua Hoyle & Sons (Bacup) Ltd, showing Bacup's three mills — India Mill (closed 1963, demolished 1972), Ross Mill (closed 1981, demolished 1982), and Plantation Mill (closed 1963, demolished 1970). (BL) INSET: Bacup 'Coat of Arms' — clogs, spindles, shuttles, and a miner's lamp, as seen just before the Great War.

Processes in the Plantation cotton Mill of Joshua Hoyle & Son, c1950.

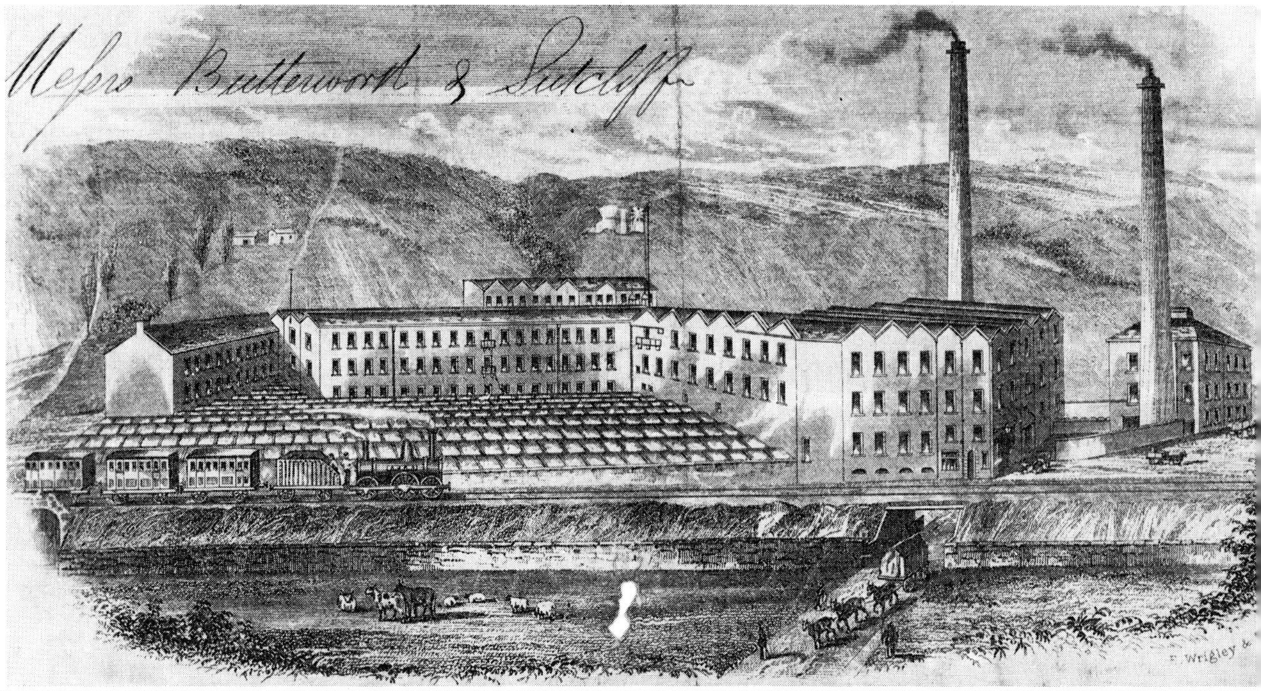
Messrs Butterworth & Sutcliffe
F. Wrigley &

COOPER St
BACUP CO-OPERATIVE SOCIETY

A COPY OF MILL RULES ISSUED BY A COTTON FIRM IN 1851

1. All the overseers shall be on the premises first and last.
2. Any person coming too late shall be fined as follows: for five minutes 2d: ten minutes 4d: fifteen minutes 6d. etc.
3. For any bobbins found on the floor, 1d. for each bobbin.
4. For single drawing, slubbing or roving 2d. for each single end.
5. For waste on the floor 2d.
6. For any oil wasted or spilled on the floor, 2d. each offence, besides paying for the value of the oil.
7. For any broken bobbins, they shall be paid for according to their value.
8. Any person neglecting to oil at the proper times shall be fined 2d.
9. Any person leaving his work and found talking with any of the other work-people shall be fined 2d. for each offence.
10. For every oath or insolent language 3d. for the first offence, and if repeated they will be dismissed.
11. The machinery shall be swept down every meal time.
12. All persons in our employ shall serve four week's notice before leaving, but (the proprietors) shall and will turn any person off without notice being given.
13. Any person wilfully or negligently breaking the machinery or damaging the brushes, making the waste fly, they shall pay for the same to the full value.
14. Any person hanging anything on the gas pendants shall be fined 2d.
15. The masters would recommend that all their people wash themselves every morning, but they shall wash themselves at least twice every week – Monday and Thursday morning and any not found washed will be fined 3d. for each offence.

OPPOSITE ABOVE: The New Bacup & Wardle Commercial Company headed notepaper showed the mills at Farholme and Kilnholme, with underpass for horses, and a train running towards the west. BELOW: Bacup Co-operative Store no 5 at Cooper Street (Underbank), early 20th century, with the butchery department next door. (BNHS) LEFT: Broadclough Mill was festooned with ivy for some 60 years until removed in 1949. The ivy was planted by John Lumb, leader of the Handbell Ringers quartette, who was head mechanic at Broadclough Mill, and spare-time gardener. David Whitehead & Sons of Rawtenstall moved into Broadclough Mill after a destructive fire which burned down their Lower Mill at Rawtenstall in November 1870. RIGHT: Rules issued by a local cotton firm in 1851. (BL) BELOW: Ross Mill, as it appeared in the 1950s; it had its own railway sidings for several years. (HO'N)

41

Footwear processes at Kilnholme Mill: ABOVE: the clicking room shows the initial cutting out of material and BELOW: the machine room, where stitching and sewing takes place. (JWJ)

LEFT: The Kilnholme lasting room, where soles are matched with uppers; RIGHT: the 'rough stuff' room, where soles are cut out, and BELOW: the finishing room, where the final articles are rounded off. (JWJ)

ABOVE: Al fresco shopping outside the market hall, and in front of the police station whose lamp can be seen on the right. (BL) BELOW: Bacup market hall: interior, date unknown. (BL)

How They Lived

The original building societies of Northern England comprised small groups of craftsmen and other workers saving regularly in order to purchase land, then build houses. In 1813 one was formed at Bacup, resulting in the building of the Club Houses, regarded as model workmen's cottages. The Club House Society laid out streets, built cottages and houses, had their own water supply, piped from an underground reservoir at Bankside, and even had their own beerhouse, the Seven Stars. They held their own weekly markets and collected tolls, their privacy being safeguarded by pillars, chains and locks, under regulations for the control of traffic made in 1856, and which remained *in situ* until 1923. The Club Houses were maintained by the Bacup Benefit Building Society until 1921, when the property was transferred to the Borough Council, under whose Housing Acts 1925-1935 most of it was demolished as the Irwell Clearance Area.

The provision of liquid refreshment was the province of pubs which flourished and attracted the young especially in the wake of the 1830 Beer Act (with licences controlled by the Board of Inland Revenue). They included one in Market Street, the 'Hark up to Nudger', which existed for some 30 years until rebuilt as the Market Hotel. The George & Dragon Inn was the hub of village life, and dated from the 16th century when much of the area was owned by the Whitakers of Broadclough Hall, to which the inn was linked by a subterranean passage.

Gas appeared in 1834, when Irwell Mill, known for a long time as 'Bottom-o-th'-Street mill' became the first in Bacup to be lit by gas, and by 1854 Bacup had 75 public gas lamps, lit from 1 October to 29 March at a charge of 21s per lamp, funded by levies raised by the churchwardens of Spotland and Newchurch. By 1869 the streets were lit from 1 September to 30 April, and by 1892 they were not extinguished until the end of May.

Meanwhile, in 1838, a report on working conditions in London highlighted the connection between insanitary conditions, disease and pauperism, and in 1839 Edwin Chadwick carried out a national survey, in which one (probably typical) Lancashire collier admitted that he never washed his body, but let his shirt rub the dirt off. Both sexes would wash their faces, necks and ears, but very seldom anywhere else. One labourer particularly remembered an event at Easter, 'because it was then he washed his feet . . .'

Chadwick's investigations were subsequently published in 1842 as the *Report on the Sanitary Condition of the labouring population*.

In March 1849 Inspector William Lee came to Bacup to make his preliminary enquiry into the general state of health. What he found was appalling. Overcrowding was common. At the 1851 Census there were 77 houses in the Temple Court area, in which lived over 500 people. One four-bedroomed house contained 13 beds and a total of 28 persons. One room contained five people in one bed, for which they paid 8d per night — 2½d for each of two adults, and 1d for each of three children. In another room six females and eight males shared four beds and, when he visited the Bacup lodging-houses after the inmates had retired to rest, most of them 'in a state of absolute nudity', he found the stench 'so obnoxious that on the following day I was scarcely able to perform my duties'.

Dr Worrall, visiting a family with fever, who had only one sleeping-room for husband, wife, six children and a male lodger, went over his shoe tops in night-soil from a privy built against the house — a back-to-back owned by Robert Munn, who did not consider the house worth repairing, but which the tenant scrupulously whitewashed every six months or so. Another family in a cellar-dwelling in Back Irwell Street (mis-named Garden Street) paid 1s a week rent, had never been well since coming to live there, and had to visit the privy at Bankhouse — fully 170 yards away.

Urchins, quite naked, were often obliged to perform their bodily excretions in the open street — and not only children but adults also — while many a dwelling was approached only by bricks across yards covered with human ordure. Things were so bad that one of the mill-owners, despairing of being able to find an unpolluted privy, had been obliged 'to skulk behind a wall'.

The River Irwell was the depository for all rubbish, waste being systematically dumped in the vain hope that the next flood would flush it away. But whenever it rained heavily, the river overflowed and flooding occurred, with catastrophic results, especially in August 1849, July 1870, and July 1881 when three lives were lost. Local shopkeepers often had to barricade their shop doors and stand on their counters when the water level rose.

The water supply was dreadful. Out of 647 houses examined, only 94 could be considered well supplied, or one house in 18 (excluding the Club Houses). Within Bacup and Lanehead, 142 houses had no water supply at all (out of a total of 213). People often had to walk over half a mile for water, queue for an hour, and then pay as much as a halfpenny for a pint potful.

Lee recommended the construction of three reservoirs — at Deerplay (considered the natural watershed for Bacup), above Heald Town, and by Scar End. The provision of a main sewer with sluices and tanks, arching over the River Irwell between Hempsteads and the Waterloo Inn, and a cemetery at a different site than one originally mooted near the Blue Ball, were commended. It took until 1862 for the cemetery to be opened at Fairwell, and even longer for other suggested improvements. Meanwhile, the death toll within a mile radius of the Mechanics' Institute during the last quarter of 1853 was double that in the healthiest parts of England at over 30 per 1,000.

Although the Rossendale Waterworks Company was established in 1853 to serve Bacup, the water supply continued to be the source of many complaints, and in 1860 only four houses were believed to have running water.

A reservoir was eventually constructed at Cowpe, nine years elapsing between the cutting of the first sod on 13 April 1901 and the official opening on 21 July 1910, due to the discovery of a geological fault between two bore holes, covered by glacial clay which could not have been easily detected.

In December 1864, Yorkshire Street still had only one privy for 20 houses. It took some Bacup people a long time to acquire the washing habit. In 1871 Edward J. Hamilton constructed a swimming bath at Grove Mill, where for 2d it was possible to indulge in the 'luxury of a wash all over'. A set of mill rules that year recommends that all employees 'wash themselves every morning, but they shall wash themselves at least twice every week. Monday and Thursday morning any not found washed will be fined 3d for each offence'. Even in 1876 a *Bacup Times* correspondent lamented the neglect of the practice of bathing. And in May 1889, when Bacup Natural History Society moved to new premises, they contained a bathroom — unusual at that time — and anyone who wanted a bath could have one for 3d if he provided his own towel, or 4d if one was supplied.

Being a poor man's child in the hungry 1840s was no joke. As a boy in Bacup, James Duckworth commented that 'even a bit of bacon was a luxury'; the staple fare was porridge and treacle or blue milk, as it was during the cotton famine. Potatoes, turnips and barley bread also figured in the daily diet, but the real necessaries of life were expensive — sugar at 7d per lb, and a 4 lb loaf of bread cost 9d or 10d.

A staple Victorian diet was flour porridge with a pat of butter and brown sugar added, followed by bread and butter and treacle (or cheese and bread). Alternatives included 'Waff' (a mixture of meal and treacle boiled like porridge), 'stir-about' (meal, bacon fat, salt and pepper, partly boiled like porridge and partly baked), while 'collop mowfin' was a cake up to 18 inches across, on which were rashers of bacon cut in wedges. Occasionally meat and fish were available (but not much of either). Suet puddings and jam roly-poly pudding were also popular, along with lobscouse — chipped potatoes boiled with a little animal food. A substitute for tea was a mixture of hyssop and pennyroyal.

Around 1855 many working-class families lived in back-to-back houses. Curtains and wallpaper were luxuries and floor-covering other than 'Irish lino' (sand) unusual. Many of the houses built by millowners for their workpeople had just two rooms, with no through ventilation. In time the typical artisan's house had a downstairs living room with scullery and one or two bedrooms above, while the better houses had a small paved yard at the back, reached by a rough back alley. Because the front door opened straight onto the street, most Bacup families used the back door: 'in Bacup you do as Bacup does, go in the back way'.

Back-to-back houses are well-known, but the most notorious of the 'top-to-bottom' houses lay along Market Street and were known as 'Plant Back'. Here a block of houses built into the steep hillside appeared from the front to be four storeys high, but really consisted of a row of two-storey houses entered from the front, and built into the hillside behind, and another row of two-storey houses on top, entered from ground level at the back — totally self-contained and separately entered.

Arthur Law, Rossendale's first Labour MP, thought Plantation Street was worse than the slums of London and the streets of Glasgow, and a running sore in the civic and social life of Bacup. Plantation Street was a long narrow cul-de-sac where only six out of 181 houses had separate exclusive toilet accommodation; Margaret Allen, who was to be hanged for murder in 1948, once resided at no 169.

A typical Bacup house in the early 20th century comprised a livingroom/kitchen lit by a single incandescent gas mantle. All cooking was done on the coal fire or in the adjoining oven, and the kettle would often be permanently bubbling away ready for whatever meal or task was due. There was no bathroom — even in 1951 60% of Bacup's houses had no fixed bathroom; there was usually just a cold water tap downstairs over a shallow stone sink under the window. Home life meant oil lamps (replenished by the lamp-oil man), and any hot water bottles were stone ones — sometimes receptacles previously used for ginger beer or sarsaparilla — and there were plenty of those, 43 mineral water manufacturers being recorded in Bacup alone.

During the 19th century, fairs were held on the Tuesday and Wednesday before Good Friday, the Friday and Saturday of Whit week, and 25-26 October, but by the end of the century there remained just the one Bacup Fair as the chief attraction during Whitsuntide, when chaos reigned supreme.

Bacup Market was established under the Public Health Act of 1848, and the foundation stone of the Market Hall was laid on Good Friday 1865 by John Dawson, Chairman of the Local Board, followed by the corner-stone the following day. It was eventually opened on 17 August 1867, covering 1,000 square yards with 39 shops and stalls, besides offices and other rooms. In 1872 a further piece of land was acquired for a drapery market, commonly known as the Rag Market. At its peak in 1913 there were 53 stalls in the Market Hall.

Bacup Market earned a reputation as one of the best markets in Lancashire for towns of comparable size. It did not close until 9 or 10 pm, being lit by naptha flares, gas light and candles.

The working-class tradition of fish and chips owes some of its impetus to the immigration of Irishmen. It appears to have begun in Bacup by 1892, in which year William Woodhouse was inviting prospective customers to 'give us a trial' at his ice cream and chipped potato restaurant at 4 Market Street and in the Market Hall. By 1897 the trade was growing, and in May the embryo Fire Service received its first summons to a fire in a fish and chip shop.

At the top of Bacup Fold was Tong Mill, alias Top o' th' Fowd. When a fire broke out in April 1870, causing £15,000 worth of damage, the only fire brigade available was the Munns' *Prince Albert*. Bacup Local Board felt that a public fire brigade was too expensive, and in any case Bacup's water supply was just not good enough. It took until 1893 for a Fire Brigade to be established, under the 1893 Police Act, the first appliance christened *The Irwell*. It gave yeoman service until replaced in 1916 by the first motor fire engine, and supplemented in June 1933 by a second engine.

St James Square used to be an island of shops — seven of them, known as the Townhead area, and bounded by Stewart Street, Yorkshire Street and Bridge Street. At no 8 Bridge Street was Marks & Spencer's Penny Bazaar, which operated for some seven years until its closure on the last day of 1920, when the Bacup branch was one of 200 to cease at that time. Across the road the odd numbers of Bridge Street are now the unchanged odd numbers of St James Square.

Bacup has never been short of public houses. In 1893 there were 79 licensed premises, one to every 297 of the population, and seven within 200 yards of Bacup centre. Eleven years later, drunkenness convictions were 8.3 per thousand population but, after the closure of 14 pubs by 1912 and a further dozen by 1924, the figure had dropped to 0.56 per thousand.

When Beatrice Potter, grand-daughter of Lawrence Heyworth, paid a clandestine visit to her maternal grandfather's native parts in November 1883, she picked her 'way along the irregularly paved and badly lighted back streets', and found Bacup people kind and considerate. She perceptively commented that 'it would be as well if politicians would live amongst the various classes they legislate for and find out . . . their wishes and ideas'. When she returned three years later, 'old Bacup remained unaltered among the bleak high hills. The mills, now busily working overtime, nestled in the valley, long unpaved streets of two-storied cottages straggling irregularly up the hills'.

On that occasion she stayed at no 5 Angel Street, a back-to-back with two bedrooms behind Providence Chapel. She felt that Bacup was 'spiritually still part of the "old world" [and] knows nothing of the complexities of modern life . . .'

The week had a regular pattern — church or chapel attendance on Sunday, washday on Monday with posser and mangle, and baking day on Thursday, when ta'toe pie or pan pie (mainly hash boiled in the porridge pan and topped with a suet crust) would be followed by rice pudding. Friday saw the weekly dusting, polishing, and donkey-stoning. Friday night was bath night, which for many families involved a zinc bath on the hearth, starting with the youngest and progressing up the age scale. It was also the night when families with a carpet would lay it down for the weekend, to be rolled up again on Sunday evening.

It was the age of the knocker-up, who was paid ½d per morning or 2d a week to awaken mill hands in time for work. Chimneys would be swept for 4d or 6d a time. Enterprising policemen trying to cope with Bank Street after heavy snowfalls would toboggan down on a shovel which would then be hauled back for its next passenger. And if lodging-houses were not whitewashed every April and October as the byelaws stipulated, there would be a fine to pay.

When a child was ill, goose grease and loving care would often work wonders. A visit to the doctor could cost half a crown — a day's wage for a working man before the Great War.

Those desperate to make domestic ends meet would do at least some of their shopping on the market after tea when things would have been reduced in price. It was a hard life — but Bacup people seemed to thrive on it.

JAMES DUCKWORTH, Limited,

THE WELL-KNOWN GROCERS, TEA, COFFEE, AND PROVISION MERCHANTS, BAKERS, &C.,

Have served the people well for many years, and still lead the way for low prices and good quality.

JAMES DUCKWORTH Limited have upwards of Fifty Branches within nine miles of Rochdale, an area with a population of about 250,000 people. Being in touch with the Best Markets, they have, by careful buying, been able to offer such value that they have won the confidence of thousands of customers.

Bread & Confectionery Department.

JAMES DUCKWORTH Limited have recently completed their NEW BAKERY IN ROCHDALE, which is admitted by experts to be the smartest and best appointed in the whole of the United Kingdom. The Bakery is lit throughout with Electricity, thus ensuring perfect cleanliness, and the Ovens and Machinery are of the very latest type. Our Bread and Confectionery will in the future be unequalled for quality and flavour, and customers will reap the advantage of years of patient study and experiment on the part of engineers to devise the most perfect method of Baking.

Tea and Coffee Department.

We sell TEAS at all prices and to suit all people but we specially recommend the three following for ordinary use:—

SHILLING TEA, 3d. per quarter (red label); ONE AND SIX TEA, 4½d. per quarter (blue label); TWO SHILLING TEA, 6d. per quarter (green label).

All our TEAS are blended to suit the local water, preserved in neat air-tight packets, and sold full weight without the packet.

Our selections of choice COFFEES from the new crop for the season include some of the finest growths of East India, Costa Rica, and Central America. Roasted on our own premises almost daily. Fresh and full of aroma.

1/-, 1/4, 1/6, 1/8, and 2/- per lb.

Note the Name: **Jas. Duckworth Ltd.**, and the Address: **Market St., and Bridge St., BACUP.**

ABOVE: James Duckworth Ltd's advert from 1897; the Market Street shop was opened in 1881 and ran for 90 years; branches at Britannia and Stacksteads closed in the 1960s. (BL) BELOW: Marks & Spencer Ltd, originators of the Penny Bazaar, had their stall at no 8 Bridge Street. This was the funeral of a Great War serviceman in 1916. The store closed at the end of 1920. (BL)

LEFT: Plantation Street before 1935 was Bacup's most notorious slum area. Some improvements took place 1935-1937, but the area was demolished in the 1960s. (PN) RIGHT: Pippin Street — cellar dwellings, with back-to-back houses above; the railway line is beyond the road. (BL) BELOW: Market Street in the 1950s — Waterworks Inn sign on left and four-storey buildings on right; these were demolished 1963-67 as part of the Market Street/Plantation Street clearance area. (HO'N)

Three Villages

Weir is the last village on the modern A671 road out of Bacup going north.

The 1754 Act creating the Rochdale & Burnley Turnpike Trust resulted in a highway ascending from Higher Broadclough up Step Row and Bacup Old Road as far as Deerplay. Hereabouts it met one of the 'Limer's Gate' paths from Sharneyford across to Heald Town and along the edge of the moor to Newkin (Nook End). Limer's Gate continues along Harrow Stiles Lane (Harrest Hills in old registers), near the end of which is a memorial stone marking the site of the Deerplay Baptist Chapel and School, 1841 and 1862.

Deerplay Hill (1,429 feet above sea level, and higher than Europa Point on Gibraltar) means 'playground of the deer', and Deerplay Inn, the sixth highest public house in England, also lays claim to the location of the highest 'bus-stop in the country at 1,126 feet. The Inn was originally known as the Stag and Hounds.

The community at Heald between 1653 and 1723 numbered 51, while Deerplay had 109. Coal was mined at Deerplay in 1612, and lead not far from Crown Point at a similar time. Deerplay (Toll) Bar was at the corner where the present A671 road meets the B6238 from Waterfoot up the Lumb Valley. On the opposite side of the road, Windy Bank turnpike served the road from Waterfoot, while travellers on the Bacup road paid their dues at the Deerplay Bar, which served as a sweet shop until the 1940s.

The name of Weir was deduced by James L. Maxim to mean 'a fence for the catching of fish' — highlighting the original importance of the River Irwell which originates in two streams rising in the fields of Irwell House Farm. Its name is probably of Anglo-Saxon origin: Erewell, the 'hoar or white spring'.

Weir also has nother name — 'Jamland', derived from the time when local families were fed on 'jam butties', consuming a thousand pots of jam a week in the process. 'T' jam colony' was a cluster of working-class houses whose inhabitants would go without jam for two months before Heald Sunday School Anniversary so that they could make a significant contribution to the collections.

Heald Town was the hub of village life about 1800 — a thriving community centred on the stone-quarrying industry. In 1841 Heald Town had a population of 107, and in 1851 167.

In 1829, a few young men working at Old Clough Mill initiated an 'Improvement Class', resulting in a Sunday School which soon outgrew its accommodation. A request to landowner James Maden of Greens resulted in the availability of a larger room at Corner (literal meaning 'a secret or confined place', possibly from the Old French *cornière*) for Baptists, Anglicans and Wesleyans together. In 1832, James Maden provided a rent-free schoolroom at Heald, on the edge of the moors; although begun as a joint venture, by the end of the year this had become purely Wesleyan. In 1867 a new Heald chapel was built of stone in the shape of a cross, and became known as the Chapel on the Moors. It survived a disastrous fire in 1932, but eventually closed for worship in the summer of 1985. The old site at Heald Town is marked by a commemorative stone erected in 1925.

In 1832 there was no mill at Weir Bottom, just a farmstead and a few cottages, with the River Irwell flowing by. Such activity as there was took place at Bent, Corner, Old Clough, and Heald Town. Bent was the name given to a row of cottages near Heald village, a few houses scattered on the edge of the moor, where rough bent grass grew down to the doors of the cottages. The present houses on Bent estate date from 1925 and were linked to the old Corner Dyeworks at Irwell Springs by a set of what are colloquially known as 'Giant's Steps'.

Old Clough Mill, operated by the Munn brothers from 1824 to 1833, was later taken over by the Irwell Springs Dyeing Company. Cotton and linen are dyed red with madder, a process borrowed from the East, leading to the description of its colour as Turkey red. The manager was Charles Henry Sieber, a naturalised Swiss, who married Joshua Hoyle's eldest daughter Alice. The Siebers gave the land for the 1867 Heald Chapel, and a few years later built Sieber Row, a row of workers' cottages colloquially known as Treacle Row; in 1878 they were renamed Clough Terrace.

By now the Siebers had left, and the Irwell Springs works were taken over by Frederick Steiner & Company, who provided gas lamps in the vicinity of their mill with the approval of Bacup Local Board, who paid £2 4s 0d for the privilege. The manager of the Turkey red dyeing process at Irwell Springs in 1881 was Robert Rankine who, with his brother John, came from Scotland in the mid-1870s, bringing with them enough soccer ability and enthusiasm to form a football team. Irwell Springs played on several different grounds successively nearer to Bacup, where they played their first match at West View on 2 September 1889, and became Bacup Football Club the following season.

When Bacup Old Band successfully competed at Belle Vue in 1864, their supporters included six enthusiasts from Weir, who on the way home decided to also form a band. The result was the Irwell Springs Band (motto: 'Instat Omnium') who entered the annual contests at Belle Vue, Manchester, in 1893, and in 1901 made their first appearance at Crystal Palace. They eventually won in 1905, repeating their success in 1908 and 1913. They were the first (and only) band to qualify for gold medals as the winners of the Crystal Palace 1,000 Guineas Challenge Trophy on three separate occasions. On four other occasions (1901, 1910, 1912, and 1925) they were runners-up. They also played 'by Royal Command' before George V in March 1914, 1921 and 1927, on each occasion at Knowsley Hall, residence of Lord Derby. They broadcast from London (August 1926) and accompanied the community singing at the only Rugby League international match ever staged at Broughton (April 1927). On all three championship occasions, the bandmaster was Walter Nuttall, who for 21 years led the band (1893-1914), later becoming Mayor of Bacup (1928-30), and a Freeman of the Borough in January 1945. When the band went out of existence in August 1960, he was the oldest surviving member.

Weir Hotel (built 1868) is the only village hostelry within the official Bacup area. The Deerplay Inn is in the Burnley licensing district, but both have been the venue for the Rossendale Hunt.

Weir possessed several coal mines. Deerplay Colliery, which lay behind Deerplay Inn, was in 1953 the only local coal mine to be modernised. At its peak it employed 250 miners and produced 80,000 tons of a coal a year. Old Clough Colliery, which closed in 1935, was reopened under private enterprise in 1952, but was closed in 1969 by the mines inspector.

A recess in the end wall of the present Weir community post office (formerly the local Co-operative store) marks the original location of a Shrine of Remembrance to villagers who fought in the Great War. Some years later a rustic cross of Scotch granite was erected on land owned by the Irwell Springs Printing Company who provided materials and site.

The south-facing Weir & District War Memorial, officially outside Bacup boundary, is an imposing landmark, and at 1,350 feet above sea-level may well be the highest monument in Britain. From here it is possible to see Blackpool Tower on a clear day, 90 degrees to the west. The memorial was unveiled in September 1935 by PC Richard Coates, the first villager to join up in the Great War. For the next 55 years members of the two churches in Weir made an annual Remembrance Day pilgrimage to lay wreaths of poppies. 139 men from the Weir district fought in the Great War, and 15 lost their lives.

The 1960s were difficult days for Weir. Their band went out of existence in 1960, Irwell Springs Printing Company ceased to function in 1964, the Deerplay Colliery closed on Friday, 13 April 1968.

In 1974 Weir Women's Institute ceased after a life of just over 20 years. Weir United football team is gone — but by no means forgotten. The sole place of worship in the village is Doals Baptist Chapel. In 1991, an application for open-cast mining on a 61-hectare site beyond the Bacup boundaries was decisively rejected by Lancashire County Council.

Today, Weir is something of a dormitory village for commuters who work elsewhere.

John Collier of Urmston, better known as the dialect writer Tim Bobbin, described Sharneyford as 't' riggin' o' th' world'. One of the highest parts of England, Sharneyford is the last outpost of Bacup before the county boundary, at 1,259 feet above sea-level. Up to the end of the 18th century, Sharneyford was little more than a hillside hamlet where sheep had long been reared, and comprised just a few houses, two quarries, and the remains of a bloomery, or iron-smelting furnace at the upper end of Saunder Clough, on a farm known as Priest-booth.

The village also marked the beginnings of Methodism in Rossendale, Heap Barn Farm on Todmorden Old Road being the venue for the first gathering of the faithful. In 1823 a preaching-place at Sharneyford came on the Methodist preaching plan, and in 1851 the Old Chapel, capacity 120, was built at a cost of £400 opposite Heap Hey Farm. Consideration was given during the 1860s to enlarging the chapel, but this never happened, and after the stoppage of Sharneyford Mill in 1880-1, and the resulting exodus of workers and their families which reduced their Sunday school from 133 to 62, the Wesleyans moved to the Board School premises where they still worship. The former Wesleyan chapel has recently been transformed into a private residence — Capella House.

Industrially, Sharneyford had the only shaft coal mines in Bacup — Tooter Hill, Blue Ball and Greave collieries each having shaft mines varying between 60 and 200 feet in depth. Hill Top colliery, begun in 1949, was the only new pit opened by the National Coal Board in Rossendale. It employed 300 men, and produced about 80,000 tons of coal a year at its peak. It closed in January 1966.

Parrock Mill was originally Park Lumb Mill, changing its name to avoid confusion with Park Mill at Britannia. This was the highest mill in England, with a chimney stack 1,200 feet above sea-level. At its peak, Parrock Mill ran 3,500 spindles and 130 looms. In 1875, the Joshua Hoyle group imported some 50 farmworkers and their families from poverty-stricken Norfolk to work in their Sharneyford Mill, also known as Heap Hey Mill. It was calculated that the population of Sharneyford from the little Primitive Methodist chapel at Change to the borough boundary at the time was nearly 500, dwelling in 185 houses. The chapel closed in 1919 and a pair of Chapel Villas built on the site.

Thomas Temperley's pipeworks functioned from 1838 to 1977, producing brown glazed pipes for sanitary ware and drainage systems. Several firms also produced bricks.

A dozen or so beer-houses opened to cater for the workers from the quarries, mines and other local industries. The Wheatsheaf and the Hop Tree Inn were both mentioned in Poor

Relief assessments; the Holy Lamb Inn is cited in 1839. Most of them have long disappeared, except for two which became private houses in Todmorden Road — Barley Mow at no 149 and Hit or Miss at nos 160-162. When the Blue Ball (formerly the Bull and Dog) closed in January 1909, its licence was transferred to the Travellers' Rest at Britannia. During the 1860s the Blue Ball was the scene of rush-bearing festivities at the September holiday weekend, which involved a footrace from that hostelry to the Toll Bar and back — and then repeated.

In March 1833, Lord Byron, the poet, who was at the time lord of the Manor of Rochdale, brought an action against James Maden of Greens and other freeholders concerning common land in the area, 143 acres of which had been enclosed by a stone wall — most of it in the Tooter Hill and Reaps Moss area. Was this part of the Manor of Rochdale or not? Though James Dearden (for Lord Byron) produced evidence of rents paid by occupiers of land in Brandwood (which included Tooter Hill and Reaps Moss), the defendants produced the Cartulary of Whalley Abbey which included the Royal edict of Edward III concerning the grant that Roger de Lacy had made to Stanlowe. This proved that the Abbot of Whalley had sold the common land of Brandwood to the freeholders before the dissolution of the monasteries in 1536, so the Crown never had a right of conveyance, and the lord of the manor had no case.

The day school at Sharneyford, erected in 1878, is still functioning, with a current official capacity of 75. The school was extended in 1993 into the disused adjoining schoolhouse.

For a few years, Sharneyford boasted a cricket team in the local league, and its own newspaper — the *Sharneyford Saturday Times and Change Leader*. During the Second World War, 103 folk from Sharneyford served in the forces, and six failed to return.

Once, Todmorden Road supported 15 mills and 26 shops. Now (1990) there are none, though there has been some housing development on the fringe of the area. One of Sharneyford's best claims to fame is its penchant for sightings of unidentified flying objects, and the Amateur Astronomy Centre over the county boundary.

A small boy in one of Bacup's outlying districts thought the song *Rule Britannia* belonged exclusively to his village. Before the turnpike road of 1754, the old highway from Bacup ran *via* Tong, Causeway House, and Trough Gate farm, joining the turnpike road at the Travellers' Rest. This formed the official boundary of Bacup, hence the queries which sometimes occur concerning houses which appear to be in Bacup but in practice are 'over the boundary'.

At the time of the Brandwood Survey of 1820 there were no dwelling-houses whatever in Britannia, though a few isolated farms existed north of the turnpike road — Higher Stack (dating from 1741), Causeway House, Hey Head, Trough Gate, and Gowther Fold. On the other side were Walmsley (dating from 1774), Deansgreave and Stubbylee Moss Farms.

By 1844 building in the area had begun — New Line, originally the Trough Gate and Lee Mill branch of the Rochdale and Burnley Trust appears, as do nine coal pits, and a factory on the site of the present Britannia Mill. The tollbar was at the junction of the old highway and the new turnpike road, on which stood Britannia Inn, built 1821 and comprising a beer-house, stable and three cottages; in 1921 it became the Britannia Working Men's Club. Most of Britannia village, named after the inn of 1821, lies on the 1,000-foot contour.

By 1869 Britannia was still described as a hamlet with one large cotton mill, where a big fire broke out in March 1886. Private fire-fighting appliances from Whitworth and Bacup brought the fire under control in 3½ hours. Ironically, at the time of the outbreak, Britannia Mill was in the process of being fitted up with fire extinguishing apparatus — which was not yet ready for use. Today, Britannia Mill is shared between the Lancashire Sock Company and Gaskells.

The Methodists were also active. Members of the Wesleyan Methodist Association (whose ministers were not as authoritarian as the Wesleyans), meeting at Waterside, regularly walked the two miles up to Britannia, where locals met to worship in a cottage at the corner of Rochdale Road and Sutcliffe Street in 1852, prior to acquiring a building familiarly known as 'Th' up steps Chapel', which later became a grocery for James Duckworth. The Wesleyans opened their premises in the summer of 1873, first a day school, which was taken over by Bacup School Board on 1 September 1894, and used for day school purposes until 2 July 1928 when the new Britannia County Primary School was opened a stone's throw away. The chapel premises were opened at the end of August 1873, capacity 400, and closed exactly 63 years later.

The foundation stones of what was now Beulah United Methodist Free Church were laid at the junction of New Line and Rochdale Road on 17 May 1884. Opened for worship in March 1885, it was destroyed by fire in October 1892, but rebuilt in 1894, when Sir James Duckworth, Rossendale-born President of the United Methodist Free Churches that year, preached at the re-opening on July 24. Beulah is now the sole place of worship in Britannia.

Henry Heys owned quarries at Britannia (said to have been the largst freestone quarry in the British Isles in 1928), Hall Cowm, and Rakehead. Britannia Quarries covered two square miles, and were in full production from 1885, leading to an old saying that 'there's gold in them there hills' — a reference to the value of the quarried materials. Here a quarryman crushed between a couple of railway wagons in 1908 managed to walk over three miles from Back Cowm Quarry home to Yate Street in Bacup, where the doctor considered that even to move him would kill him. He died about 7 o'clock that same evening, a typical local 'brownback' who would never admit being badly hurt.

Meanwhile, the long-delayed railway extension had opened in 1881, thus providing Britannia with the highest station on the Lancashire and Yorkshire branch of the railway. The station closed as an economy measure on 2 April 1917, thirty years before the Bacup-Rochdale line ceased altogether as far as passenger services were concerned; but in January 1940 the last train from Rochdale to Bacup was marooned at Britannia and remained snowbound for five days.

The area has now been landscaped as part of the Britannia Greenway and on the Shawforth side of Deansgreave Bridge by Whitworth UDC in 1971. Britannia had three cotton mills and three pubs, of which the Wellington Hotel (twinned with Club Ewaldi in Bocholt since 1952), and the Travellers' Rest still remain.

Britannia's biggest claim to fame is provided by the Britannia Coconut Dancers of Bacup (their official title), who every Easter Saturday start from the Travellers' Rest about 9 am, dance their way round Fairview estate, and reach Bacup centre about noon. After lunch and a tour of town centre pubs, they continue dancing down to Stacksteads, concluding at the Glen around 7 pm. During the day they will have covered about 65 miles and worn out a full set of clog irons.

The dancing tradition previously carried on by the Tunstead Mill troupe moved after the Great War to Britannia, where quarryman Arthur Bracewell senior, Fred Gregory and James Mawdsley, a former Tunstead Mill dancer who had moved to Britannia, resurrected the tradition. The first performance of the newly-formed Britannia Coconut Dancers took place at Burnley on Good Friday 1925, and the following day they danced their way from the Dog & Partridge at Stacksteads up to Bacup centre, concluding at the Working Men's Club at Britannia.

The dancers were perhaps at the height of their local popularity in the 1950s, when the team's first TV appearance 'brought prestige to Bacup in general and the village of Britannia in particular'. Until 1961, the 'Nutters' performed on Good Friday as well as Easter Saturday but, owing to the risk of their garlands being ruined by bad weather on Good Friday, their principal dancing day is now Easter Saturday, together with the local Carnival day (usually late June) and other special occasions. Their route has started from Britannia since 1964.

The Women's Institute in Britannia ran for just under 20 years from March 1959 to the end of November 1978. Britannia United football team had some success in the Rochdale & District Amateur League.

Today, Britannia appears to have gone almost full circle: no coal mines (where once there were about 16), and little industry, but plenty of good quality housing for people who commute elsewhere to earn their living.

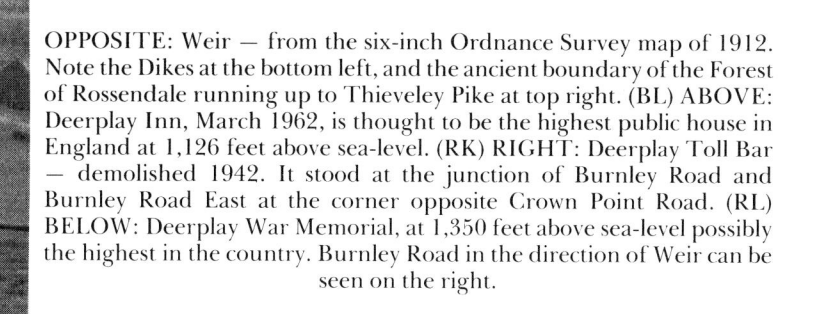

OPPOSITE: Weir — from the six-inch Ordnance Survey map of 1912. Note the Dikes at the bottom left, and the ancient boundary of the Forest of Rossendale running up to Thieveley Pike at top right. (BL) ABOVE: Deerplay Inn, March 1962, is thought to be the highest public house in England at 1,126 feet above sea-level. (RK) RIGHT: Deerplay Toll Bar — demolished 1942. It stood at the junction of Burnley Road and Burnley Road East at the corner opposite Crown Point Road. (RL) BELOW: Deerplay War Memorial, at 1,350 feet above sea-level possibly the highest in the country. Burnley Road in the direction of Weir can be seen on the right.

LEFT: Walter Nuttall (1867-1962), bandmaster of Irwell Springs Band, was a native of Weir, worked in the mills for 37 years until he was 47 when he became a professional band instructor. He conducted Goodshaw Band and Stacksteads (as the Home Guard Band) during the 1939-45 World War. RIGHT: Weir Post Office, formerly the Co-operative Society building; in the recess at the side was the original War Memorial which was later superseded by the landmark on Deerplay Hill. BELOW: Irwell Springs Band's first Royal Command performance was in 1914. Two further Command performances followed — 17 March 1921 and 27 March 1927. (BNHS)

Sharneyford — from the 25-inch Ordnance Survey map of 1930, and
INSET: Toll Bar House, Sharneyford, still occupied as a private house.
(BNHS)

ABOVE: Britannia Station and staff — date unknown; the station closed in 1917. (HO'N) BELOW: Britannia from the Ordnance Survey map of 1911.

ABOVE: Troughgate, Britannia, at the turn of the century; there are no tramlines yet, and nothing beyond two rows of stone-fronted houses.
BELOW: Britannia — aerial view taken 1973. (JH)

LEFT: Henry Maden (1828-1890), local mill-owner and magistrate owned 415 acres of land in Bacup. RIGHT: John Henry Maden, Bacup's best-known and perhaps wealthiest benefactor, was President of many local societies, a local and county councillor, and MP for Rossendale 1892-1900 and 1917-18. (RL) BELOW: St Saviour's day school was built in 1858 to accommodate 662 pupils. Its condemnation in February 1982 and subsequent demolition expedited the review of Bacup primary schools. (AH)

Bacup's Benefactors

In St Saviour's Parish Church tower is a full peal of eight bells, installed to celebrate the Golden Jubilee of Queen Victoria in 1887. The principal subscribers were Henry Maden, James Maden Holt, Edward Hoyle and Miles Ashworth. Each had his name inscribed on a bell, and each has a place in the munificent history of Bacup.

Henry Maden, of Rockcliffe House, was the son of John Maden (1800-1869), who initiated the firm of John Maden & Son. As a boy John Maden wove woollen cloth on a handloom and, when he married at the age of 20, he and his wife 'had not a pound to bless us with'. But after working at Ormerods' woollen mill at Waterbarn, he set up in business with Joshua Hoyle (1796-1859), Richard Bridge and Daniel Baron in 1834, before becoming a mill-owner in his own right in 1837 when he bought Throstle Mill, and built Oak House as his residence — a building later used by John Maden & Son as offices. By 1851 he was employing 145 workers, and as he prospered, he rented Lee Mill from J. M. Holt of Stubbylee, built Springholme Mill, and purchased the manor of Raw Cliffe Wood, on which he built Rockcliffe House — the name being a corruption of Raw Cliffe. John Maden became one of Bacup's first 'cotton lords', investing his profits in collieries (he owned two in Bacup), rail-roads, farmlands in Bacup and Haslingden Grane, and shipping on Tyneside.

His son Henry was born at Fearns on 15 October 1828, and worked in his maternal grandfather's grocery business until his father took him into partnership as John Maden & Son. After his father's death in January 1869, Henry took sole control of the business, and in May 1869 was elected a magistrate. He felt Bacup needed somewhere for boys to go to play, rather than 'be brought up before this bench for creating a nuisance' by playing in the streets. He often imposed fines on young offenders — and afterwards paid them himself.

In 1871 Henry Maden became a director and the largest subscriber in the ill-fated Troy Silver Mining Company, who named a tunnel at their Nevada site after him. He was also a shareholder in the Bacup Co-operative Store, and in 1874 when the local Liberals bought the house and shop formerly used as a Co-operative Store, he 'assisted in his usual liberal manner'.

In 1888 he financed a Maden Scholarship, making £50 available for children from working-class homes to study for a year at Owens College — opportunities not otherwise available. The first student to be awarded a Maden Scholarship was a young weaver named Herbert Bolton, who in 1890 published the standard *Geology of Rossendale,* and in 1898 became Curator of the Bristol Museum.

He was a keen and shrewd businessman with an eye and a memory for detail. At one Bacup Council meeting, he challenged one account as being 'not according to contract'. When the tender was checked, it was found that the item in question had been charged *threepence* more than the contract price.

Henry Maden had a son long before he got married on his 46th birthday in 1874. The youngster's birth was never officially registered, and John Henry Kay lived with his natural mother in Salford, attending Manchester Grammar School during the 1870s before becoming a salesman in the Manchester office of the family business. In June 1889, Henry Maden purchased farms at Bankside, Top o' th' Bank, and Slip Inn, anticipating that part of the farmland should be used as a public recreation ground, but died on 21 September 1890, leaving estate valued at £327,193 19s 6d nett, and a reputation as an impartial magistrate and a provident steward.

His son, who had in 1885 changed his name by deed poll to John Henry Maden, inherited his father's looks and outlook, and during 1893 gave the land for the new Liberal Club, presented the Maden Recreation Grounds (official size five acres, two roods and 26 perches) at Bankside, and on 16 December the Maden Public Baths were opened in Rochdale Road, the cost having tripled to £12,000 from the original estimate in 1890. As a result, John Henry Maden was elected the first Freeman of the Borough of Bacup.

When elected to Parliament in 1892, he introduced a bill to restrict working hours in the cotton trade to eight hours a day, a move which failed, though he tried to implement it in his own mills; his employees were afraid that a shorter working week would reduce their earnings. In 1895 he was elected to Bacup Council, became the youngest Mayor to date in 1896-7, and was re-elected to that office in November 1900, serving as Mayor throughout the Edwardian era. He became Bacup's first motorist, driving a Rolls Royce registration number K 4821, and continued his father's custom of entertaining the poorer old people of the district to Christmas dinner and tea.

The Madens also financed a visit from Helen Porter Mitchell on behalf of the Bacup Sick Nursing Society. Miss Mitchell, better known as Dame Nellie Melba, visited the Royal Court Theatre on 6 February 1911. Programmes cost 6d each; seats in the dress circle were 21s each (more than a week's pay for many townspeople), orchestral stalls 10s 6d each, and standing room tickets were issued at 2s each. The Bacup Sick Nursing Society received the entire proceeds, amounting to £272 13s 6d.

In September 1912, a drinking fountain built of Aberdeen granite was erected at a cost of £750 as a public memorial to the Maden family. Originally sited atop the recently covered-over River Irwell in Bacup centre, the memorial was transferred to Stubbylee Park in 1923. The two allegorical figures at each of the top corners represented education and knowledge in the case of Henry Maden, charity and enterprise in the case of his son.

Sir Henry Maden (as he preferred to be known) was knighted in June 1915, and died of cancer at the age of 58 on 18 February 1920. His widow outlived him for 30 years, and son Henry (Hal), who had no interest in the cotton trade, became a lawyer and died childless in November 1960.

James Maden Holt was similarly to implement the wishes of *his* father, John Holt (1804-1856), who married into the family of James Maden of Greens (1766-1849), whose family line dates back to at least 1703 when James Maydin of Broadclough was one of the Overseers of the Poor. By 1810, James Maden, cotton mill-owner and philanthropist, owned 30 acres of land and at least two coal pits. He was also a staunch evangelical, and one of a group of five clergy and five laymen who initiated a Bacup branch of the British and Foreign Bible Society.

His marriage to the daughter of one of the Whitworth Doctors was blessed with seven children, and their third daughter Judith married John Holt of Stubbylee on 25 June 1828. The Holt estates originally covered all the south side of the River Irwell from Cowpe across Brandwood Moor to Shawforth and thence to Sharneyford.

John Holt, whose mother was Anne Heyworth of Greensnook Hall, became Bacup's second magistrate (and the first for the Salford Hundred) in April 1838. As an *ex-officio* member of the Poor Law Guardians, he was a target for the resentment felt by unemployed handloom weavers at government attempts to eliminate outdoor relief. One dark February evening in 1843 a shot was fired, probably intended for him. The would-be assassin was never found, despite a £200 reward being offered for the arrest and conviction. John Holt was unharmed, but his wife Judith, already ill, was terrified, and died of influenza three weeks later at the age of only 38.

John Holt died in 1856, leaving two children — James Maden Holt and Emily Sarah Holt, the latter a prolific writer of novels with an evangelical bias, set in times of religious crisis. They had been raised within the strict evangelical regime of the Madens, and James Maden Holt remained a rigid Protestant all his life. In 1868 he became the first Bacup-born local MP when the new North-East Lancashire constituency was formed, devoting his maiden speech to the folly of disestablishing the Protestant Church in Ireland. He held the seat in 1874 against the challenge of the Marquis of Hartington, a member of the Cavendish family of Chatsworth Park.

His father had always intended to provide a local church for the members of the working class in the area, who had begun to worship in an old mill at Rockliffe in 1854. Between 1858 and 1865 St Saviour's school, vicarage, and church were built on James Maden Holt's own land, at his own expense, with stone from his own quarries. On completion he deposited £300 with a church building society, some of the interest from which helped to repair the 150-foot spire in February 1975.

St Saviour's is one of the few Anglican churches in England with a baptistery for total immersion. Sunk into the chancel floor between the choir stalls, and covered by an ornamental grating, the area is normally carpeted and therefore undetected by the casual visitor, but the baptistery is unique in the Manchester diocese.

The longest-serving Vicar was Rev William Johnson, Vicar for 47 years until his death on 7 December 1916. An uncompromising evangelical, he favoured the black preaching gown which he always wore in the pulpit, but terrified children in the day-school by teaching them that if they were good they would go to Heaven, but if they were bad they would go in the burning fire for ever and ever . . .

During the cotton famine of 1862/5, James Maden Holt found work for many unemployed male cotton operatives, constructing a 'Cotton Panic Road' behind Height Barn Farm and through Lee Quarries over Brandwood Higher Moor, intending to drain the moor and build farms up there, but the depth of moorland peat and gorse meant that the scheme was never completed, and the road petered out.

When he died on 18 September 1911, J. M. Holt bequeathed Stubbylee Hall and grounds to Bacup. The borough surveyor had already been instructed to plan for the adaptation of Stubbylee Hall 'for municipal offices to accommodate all the departments of the Corporation' — a move which became actuality in 1920.

Stubylee Park was presented by the trustees of Miles Ashworth (1827-1889), not to be confused with his namesake from Cowpe (1849-1924) who became Mayor of Rochdale. By his father's marriage, he too was descended from the Heyworths of Greensnook. In June 1885 he presented the mayoral robe to Bacup Council.

When Queen Victoria celebrated her Golden Jubilee in 1887, all the local Sunday Schools marched in procession, each child being given a commemorative medal. One group marched to Britannia and back to Acre Mill House, where Miles Ashworth gave each of them an orange. 25 years after his death, his trustees presented Stubbylee Park to Bacup Corporation

Corporation in December 1914 for the benefit and enjoyment of the inhabitants of the borough. The cost of the park from the Stubbylee estate was £2,832, and 'the clear yearly income of the Charity shall be applied ... towards defraying the cost of laying out, ornamenting and maintaining the Stubbylee and Moorlands Park and Recreation Ground at Bacup'.

The refreshment kiosk in Stubbylee Park was financed from the residuary estate of former Brandwood Councillor John Howorth, and built with stone from the old barn which stood across from Fearns Hall until its demolition in December 1975.

Edward Hoyle (1834-1897), fifth son of Joshua Hoyle, Bacup's first 'cotton lord', lived in Moorlands House, a stone mansion built in 1870, and followed his father as head of Joshua Hoyle & Sons. In 1871 he employed 1,600 workers. He was a keen businessman, a generous supporter of missionary enterprises, and was never willingly absent from Sunday worship at Wesley Place. After his death in 1897 and that of his widow 15 years later, his son Joshua (who in May 1892 added his maternal grandfather's surname and became Joshua Craven Hoyle therafter) and other members of the family presented Moorlands Park to the Borough of Bacup in June 1914 for the benefit and enjoyment of the inhabitants. Moorlands House was demolished in 1914 to make way for the Italian garden in Moorlands Park, and Moorlands Terrace was built from the stone.

James Smith Sutcliffe (1834-1891) marked his mayoral year by offering to buy up the Townhead property, so that the narrow and dangerous streets there could be widened and improved — a move for which the public were not yet ready.

Two years after his death in January 1889, Dr Joseph Hardman Worrall was being hailed as a forgotten benefactor. A pioneer of local government in Bacup, he was a member of the Local Board from its formation in 1863 (and Chairman from 1875), their un-paid medical officer, and for 43 years was Bacup's best-loved family doctor. If people could not pay, he never charged for either attendance or medicine, and if necessary would sit all night by the bedside of a desperately sick person. Quiet and unassuming, he was an early donor to the Bacup Mechanics' Institute prize fund, and gave much financial help to Bacup Natural History Society. The tallest monument in Bacup Cemetery, a granite obelisk 18½ feet high, commemorates his 'deep interest in the physical, social, and intellectual welfare of the inhabitants of Bacup'. 'His motto was "Deeds not Words"'.

And that serves as an appropriate epitaph to many other benefactors of Bacup, to whom the town owes so much.

LEFT: James Maden Holt (1829-1911), owner of Stubbylee Hall, donor of St Saviour's school, vicarage, and church. (AH) RIGHT: Edward Hoyle (1834-1897), son of Joshua Hoyle, mill-owner; philanthropist and benefactor of Bacup. (BL) BELOW: James Smith Sutcliffe (1834-1891), businessman, magistrate, donor of the Bacup mayoral chain, and underwriter of *Joyful News*. (BNHS)

BACUP, February 25th, 1812.

AT A
RESPECTABLE MEETING
OF THE
INHABITANTS OF THIS VILLAGE,
And its Vicinity,

To take into Consideration the Propriety of establishing a Society,

IN AID OF THE

British and Foreign
BIBLE SOCIETY,
IN LONDON,

It was unanimously resolved:—

I. THAT the present meeting do highly approve the plan and objects of the British and Foreign Bible Society.

II. THAT an auxiliary society be formed, consisting of the inhabitants of this village and its vicinity, to be denominated the AUXILIARY BIBLE SOCIETY of BACUP.

III. That this society adopt, as far as possible, the rules and regulations of the parent society in London.

IV. That this society correspond with the parent institution through the medium of the Manchester society.

V. That a Committee be formed, to carry these resolutions into immediate effect, consisting of

Rev. WILLIAM PORTER,	Mr. MADEN, *Greens*,
Rev. THOMAS COOPER,	Mr. G. ORMEROD, *Green's Nook*,
Rev. JOSEPH CHAPMAN,	Mr. J. WHITAKER, jun. *Broad-clough*,
Rev. JOHN HIRST,	Mr. E. LORD, *Bacup*,
Rev. THOMAS KING,	Mr. J. EARNSHAW, jun. *Bacup*.

VI. That the resident Ministers of Bacup, of every denomination, subscribing in aid of this society, shall be of the Committtee and entitled to a vote.

VII. That Mr. HEYWORTH be appointed President and Secretary, and Mr. JAMES WHITAKER, jun. Treasurer, to this society.

VIII. That Shrove-Tuesday be the day appointed for the annual meeting of the members of this society, and that the Committee shall give timely and public notice where the said meeting shall be held.

IX. That the Committee be empowered to call the society together at such other times as they may deem necessary.

X. That every member of this society exert himself in soliciting contributions and subscriptions from his neighbours and friends, and remit the same, when obtained, to the Treasurer.

XI. That each subscriber of half-a-guinea annually shall be a member.

Poster advertising a meeting regarding an auxiliary Bible Society of Bacup in 1812. (RC)(I)

LEFT: Programme cover for the visit of Dame Nellie Melba on 6 February 1911 to Bacup Court Theatre; her visit was funded by the Madens. RIGHT: Dr Joseph Hardman Worrall (1824-1889), Bacup's medical benefactor, and son of a Wesleyan minister, is shown in characteristic pose. BELOW: St Saviour's Church interior; the baptistery, the only one in the Manchester diocese (formed 1847), is below the carpet in the chancel; 1985. (AH)

£200.
REWARD

WHEREAS,

On the Evening of Wednesday last, the 22nd Instant,

AN ATTEMPT WAS MADE

TO ASSASSINATE

Mr. John Haworth, on his approach to Stubbylee, near Bacup, the Residence of John Holt Esq., by

FIRING A PISTOL

AT HIM.

The above Reward will be paid by the Government to any Person who shall give such Information and Evidence as will lead to the discovery and conviction of the Party or Parties engaged in the attempt.

And HER MAJESTY'S GRACIOUS PARDON will be granted to an Accomplice, not being the Person who ACTUALLY FIRED THE PISTOL, WHO SHALL GIVE SUCH EVIDENCE as shall lead to the same result.

Information to be given to CAPTAIN WOODFORD, Chief Constable, Preston; Mr. PHENIX, Superintendent of Police, at Rochdale; Mr. Mc. CABE, Superintendent of police, at Burnley; or to Sergeant FARRADY, at Bacup.

Constabulary Office, February 25th, 1843.

J. DOWNHAM, PRINTER, BOOKSELLER, &c. BACUP.

Poster regarding an assassination attempt on 22 February 1843; Sergeant Farrady was Bacup's first policeman under the 1839 Lancashire Constabulary. (RC)(I)

Stacksteads

When Victoria became Queen in 1837, there was not a single place of worship in Stacksteads. It was simply a village, and was not even known by that name.

In 1338, the Abbot of Whalley, who held the land on lease, was complaining about trespassers on his grass at Tunstead — one of the five Rossendale vaccaries along the upper reaches of the River Irwell, and let out to farmers in 1342, at which time pastures at 'Settynges and Soclogh' (Sedges and Sowclough) were linked to the vaccary at Tunstead, literal meaning 'a farmstead' (*tun-stide*). The 1507 Copyholder's Survey of the Forests or Chases of Blackburnshire includes 'a Vaccary callid TUNSTED', the tenants of which were twenty years later paying copyhold rents proportionate to the size of their holdings — 6s 8d, 13s 4d, or 26s 8d per person. In October 1534 the Halmot Court divided Sedges and Sowclough into two parts, eastern and western, stipulating 'that there should be a way between them . . . from le Kyrkesteid to le Stacksted . . .' This appears to be the first mention of Stacksteads, a name derived from *stagsteads* (animals).

A local legend indicates that the mother church of the area might have been built at Tunstead, had not the building materials assembled there on each of three separate occasions been spirited away to Newchurch, where the proposed edifice was then built (1511).

Early maps show that Tunstead was nominally a subdivision of Tunstead and Wolfenden Booth — just over 626 acres on the northern side of the River Irwell. The southern side of the river was Brandwood Lower End, which belonged to the parish of Rochdale.

The Newchurch parish registers from 1653 to 1723 show that there were a mere eight residents in Stacksteads, though at Fearns there were 41, up Rakehead 48, and at Greens 46.

Tunstead possesses two of the oldest buildings in Rossendale. One is Fearns Hall, parts of which originally dated from 1557, though the earliest visible datestone is over the porch of 1646. The other is the recently renovated Waggoner Tunstead, which lies on the old packhorse road and dates from 1632.

Round the corner was the former Haslingden Union Workhouse at Mitchellfield Nook, first mentioned in 1733 as 'the Bacup Poorhouse'. From 1744 it was known as the 'Briggclough Poorhouse', but from 1756 is often called Tunstead Poorhouse — and survived until the last quarter of the 19th century. Originally built as a handloom weaving shop, the workhouse became an accommodation centre for the homeless. When the Haslingden Poor Law Union was formed in 1838, the workhouse was overcrowded with 200 inmates, most of them pauper weavers. Although by 1841 there were only 36 inmates, an inspection in March 1847 found the place defective, with no provision for isolating infectious cases, and in May 1848 a married couple aged 40 and their two children were sharing one bed. In 1851 there were 17 men, 19 women and seven children, and in 1861, 45 women, two men and three children, but by 1870 Pikelaw had been built on the Haslingden/Rawtenstall border, after which the Tunstead Poorhouse ceased to function as such.

The farm at Mitchellfield Nook comprised an area of over 34 acres, and from March 1755 was subject to a yearly rent of 2s payable at Christmas, permitting the landlord to carry away manure, compost and ashes. In the same area is Honey Hole, which owed its name to some beehives kept at Wolfenden Booth by a mediaeval priest.

Fern Hill House was built by George Ormerod, woollen manufacturer, who married the sister of Justice Whitaker of Broadclough Hall. After the Ormerods moved into Edgeside Hall in 1863, Fern Hill was successively occupied by James Munn, magistrate and cotton spinner (drowned on 22 July 1871 when his boat, the *Emily,* sank during the Lytham Regatta), and his sister Margaret Alice, who in 1876 married William Mitchell (1838-1914), eldest son of a Fearns Hall woollen manufacturer. William Mitchell became Conservative MP for Burnley (1900-1906), and was also Vicar's Warden at Tunstead Church.

During the Great War, Fern Hill House served as an auxiliary hospital for invalided convalescent soldiers. Members of the Nursing Division of St John Ambulance Brigade gave one week in three to help, and men not called up for the Forces did night duty. But the nurses never put on bandages nor saw a wound dressed — they simply cleaned up, washed windows, and kept the home fires burning. Between November 1914 and February 1919 a total of 738 patients passed through Fern Hill Military Hospital — which had 25 beds, supplemented by a further 50 at Acre Mill Baptist School. After briefly reverting to private ownership, the house was demolished in the late 1920s, and the area redeveloped as the Fernhill estate.

Heath Hill House was built by the Munn family who were of Scottish origin, and often returned there for hunting and shooting purposes. In fact Robert Munn's two younger daughters were born in Scotland, and in 1881, when his son Robert Whittaker Munn had become the head of the family, all five family servants were of Scottish origin. R. W. Munn died on 15 September 1890 at the age of only 46; his son eventually left to serve in the Forces, and the house was taken over by Dr Eric Walter Falconer, son of the then Vicar of Tunstead. His youngest son Francis also became a doctor in Stacksteads.

Churches came in fairly rapid succession in the early Victorian era. The Baptists and Wesleyan Methodists arrived in the late 1830s, the former as a result of conversions due to the preaching of Irwell Terrace pastor Rev Thomas Dawson. Orchard Hill was opened on St Swithin's Day 1838, but on the 1844 map is shown as Road End Baptist Church, 250 yards from the Tunstead Toll Bar and on the old turnpike road linking Rooley Moor and Windy Bank. It became known as Waterbarn when new premises were opened at Christmas 1847. Their longest-serving minister was Rev John Howe, pastor 1851-1887.

John Wesley is reputed to have preached at Sissclough, but the first certain mention of Wesleyan Methodism is a society class at Sowclough, which led to a chapel on the site later occupied by Stacksteads station signalbox. A second chapel in premises which later became the Co-operative Store was followed by the first Stacksteads Wesleyan chapel, opened in 1872. The earlier chapels were both named Tunstead.

Robert Hamer, better known as 'Bury Bob', a quarryman at Frost Holes, and the most notorious drunkard in Stacksteads, had been guilty of virtually everything but murder. By the time he was 34, he had been to prison 26 times, and had been dubbed a walking cutler's shop, because of the numbers of pocket knives and penknives he had swallowed for wagers. At the end of February 1881, it was reported that a quarryman, with his hands tied behind his back, had been fighting a bulldog named Joe; the story was embellished and exaggerated in the national press, and led to the Home Secretary directing the Chief Constable of Lancashire to inquire into the affair. Then in June 1882, under the inspired preaching and praying of the Wesleyan lay paastor, Samuel Chadwick, Bury Bob was soundly converted, and remained so until his death on 27 January 1887.

The Primitive Methodists were active on the Old Road, where their original premises are today known as Chapel Cottages. They eventually merged with their Wesleyan counterparts in 1952, their Booth Road premises being struck by a devastating thunderbolt on 5 June 1982, and demolished during the summer of 1983.

Three local magistrates and landowners (Robert Munn of Heath Hill, George Ormerod of Fern Hill, and John Holt of Stubbylee) became the first trustees of Holy Trinity Church, Tunstead, whose first services were held on Guy Fawkes Day 1840. 'Parson Haworth' was the longest-serving Vicar, from 1851 to 1889, and superintended the building of the new Tunstead Schools which were opened on Guy Fawkes Day 1881. Before 1880 the day school, now the only Church-controlled school in Bacup, was housed in what became Tunstead Mission and Men's Institute, and remained so until the outbreak of World War II. They subsequently became a slipper works.

Another Mission was St Luke's, in 'temporary' premises of corrugated iron on Holme Street, which in practice did service for the whole of the mission's active life (1894-1968), holding services on Sunday afternoons so as not to clash with Tunstead Mission, whose services were held in the evening.

The question of Easter dues, or the 'Vicar's rate', was a sore point among a largely nonconformist population. Technically a rent charge, the fact that church rates were charged on every property owner led to great opposition, stronger in Rochdale and Rossendale than anywhere else. It came to a head in Stacksteads when shopkeeper Richard Cunliffe of Tunstead Bottom, secretary to the Anti-Easter Dues Association, flatly refused on principle to pay the levy of eleven pence. When the Vicar of Whalley's local representative gave notice that his goods and chattels would be distrained and sold in order to meet not only the 11d for Easter dues but a further 10s costs, Cunliffe displayed the relevant documents outside his shop, virtually across the road from Tunstead Church, and in effect dared the authorities to do their worst. In practice, nothing more was heard of the matter, and seven years later, the Compulsory Church Rate Abolition Act of 1868 made all church rates voluntary.

The earliest mill at Stacksteads was built in 1700 at Waterbarn, for which Lawrence Ormerod was assessed 5s in 1751. There have been many changes of ownership, but in June 1893 news of a fire at Waterbarn Mill was relayed to the police station by a rail traveller, as a result of which the Chief Constable pleaded for telephonic communication with the outlying parts of the borough.

Industries grew, and the navvies who helped to build the railways stayed to work the quarries. Frost Holes, also known as Law Bottom, was one of many, and lay south of the railway behind Stacksteads station, adjoining Stacksteads brickworks and the tramway which linked Richard Siddall's stone siding with Greens Moor quarry on the hills. In January 1879 several children at Tunstead school had 'difficulty in finding school pence owing to quarrymen being out of work through frost', and a severe frost three years later lasted nearly two months.

Stacksteads had nine coal pits, the last to cease operations being Stacksteads Colliery (The Hile), which closed in September 1946 after 125 years. It was linked to the coal staithe at the Toll Bar by a chain road or tramway. In the garden of Honey Hole farm was a scarecrow, which was the target for colliers traversing the nearby bridge with their tubs of coal. All the farmer had to do was pick up the coal later . . .

Boggart Hole Clough, officially known as Folly Clough, ran from Higher Tunstead to the Hare & Hounds at Lower Tunstead. At the junction of Rook Hill and the 'Old Road' was Syke Foundry (also known as Boggart Foundry), which closed in the 1870s, and was later used as a size works.

In business at Syke Foundry was John Atherton (1820-1863), who in 1860 built the last of the cotton co-operatives on land at Lower Holme and named it Rossendale Mill — but it has always been knwn as Atherton Holme.

Meanwhile, Stacksteads population was growing — from 2,114 in 1841 to 3,703 in 1851, when 603 houses were occupied, and some 58 tradesmen or shopkeepers were in business. By 1861 there were 1,275 houses with 6,263 occupants, and a similar figure in 1871 was enough to increase the total population of Bacup by 30% when the 'west end' was annexed in 1876. By this time there were 800 ratepayers in Stacksteads and the rateable value was £5,251 5s. In 1879 the total population of the ecclesiastical district of Tunstead was 6,325, and at the 1881 Census the village of Stacksteads reached its population peak at 7,701.

Sanitation was deplorable, the proportion of privies being no better than in Bacup in 1849, so that fever and diarrhoea were frequent. In 1882 the *Bacup Times* suggested that Stacksteads was 'one of the places needing progress most'.

Tunstead Mill is a name loosely given to the area from below the Wesleyan chapel to the Glen, which gave rise to the principal musical and literary leisure activities.

There were three separate Tunstead Mills, the second being the one visited by the loom-breakers, and the third being built in 1850. This was occupied for 23 years by Turnbull & Stockdale as Irwell Bank Printworks, and from 1908 to 1936 by Riding & Gillow, bleachers and finishers.

Tunstead Mill coconut dancers were all quarrymen, with a fondness for large quantities of alcoholic beverages. The troupe, active from 1857 until the outbreak of the Great War, in which many of them were killed, comprised eight adult men, wearing costume identical to that sported by the Britannia 'Nutters' today. They performed annually on Good Friday and Easter Saturday. Other performances were rare.

Stacksteads Amateur Brass Band developed out of the pre-1872 Tunstead Boys' Church Band early in 1872 when they visited Waterbarn Band of Hope. Thanks to Henry Maden, they had paid all debts and acquired instrumental music within two years. The band won the first prize at the Westhoughton Band contest in 1908-9-10, thus earning the right to designate themselves as a Prize Band, and are the only Bacup band to reach their centenary.

Stacksteads Literary Institute, established 1869, subsequently became the Conservative Club, opening as such on 28 May 1881, the year that Benjamin Disraeli died. In 1941 the Club was renamed after Disraeli's peerage title: the Beaconsfield Conservative Club. There was also a Liberal equivalent, which met in premises now utilised as a handyman's shop.

The eastern part of Stacksteads was Acre Mill — an area which a century ago comprised one Baptist school-chapel (opened 1871 to fill a Baptist gap between Zion and Waterbarn chapels), one woollen mill (employing 100 at its peak), and three cotton mills: Acre Mill — which had the telephone number Bacup 1, Farholme, and Victoria.

In Herbert Street was the Premier Skating Rink, which was also used for ice hockey until the Olympia Picture Palace took over just before the Great War, during which the premises became a 'British' clog factory. On Armistice Day 1929 it again became, briefly, a roller-skating rink, until Schofield's took over the premises for a bakery which is still familiarly known by their name.

Between the wars, half the mills in Stacksteads changed from cotton manufacture to footwear, including Stacksteads Mill, which was operated from 1928 until 1990 by the Bacup Shoe Company. In 1922 the Lancashire Footwear Manufacturers Association was set up as a collective buying organisation, forming the Valley Supply Company which took over Farholme Mill after the Bacup and Wardle Commercial Manufacturing Company was wound up in 1928.

When the idea of a recreation ground was first mooted at Stacksteads, the primary motive was that young men of the area had nothing to do. This was in 1897. Nearly a century later a grandiose scheme envisages a five-a-side astro-turf football pitch behind the Rose 'n' Bowl, which was itself converted into a restaurant in December 1990 after having been the Stacksteads Working Men's Club for 108 years. A sketch map shows the historical pattern of this area.

The image of Stacksteads has improved considerably in recent years, and its future seems bright.

The old workhouse at Mitchell Field Nook, depicted 1902, and originally dating from the 1730s; parts remain and are private residences.

ABOVE: Tunstead Mill coconut dancers celebrate their jubilee in 1907. (BNHS) BELOW: Honey Hole, Stacksteads, c1900, with the tramway from Stacksteads Colliery to the coal staithe at the bottom of Booth Road. The houses on the skyline are at Stoney Hill. (HO'N)

ABOVE: How the *Illustrated Police News* saw the fight between quarryman Robert Hamer and a bulldog called Joe in February 1881; the postal address of Stacksteads at the time was 'near Manchester'. BELOW: Tunstead Mission room became a footwear factory during the 1940s. Bacup Shoe Company's factory at Atherton Holme is behind, with part of the Taylor Holme industrial estate.

ABOVE: Premier Skating Rink, Herbert Street, Stacksteads, Christmas in the 1890s; the premises have served several purposes since — picture palace, skating rink (again), clog factory and bakery. BELOW: Tunstead Mill, general view c1900, shows the railway, Wesleyan chapel and several mills. (BL)

LEFT: The Glen c1913; rail, river, and road with tramcar, and Baxter's Brewery, whose chimney was raised to 192 feet in order to avoid the unusual air currents in the Glen, and RIGHT: in 1993, showing road and river, with the railway tunnel, now part of the Irwell Valley walkway. BELOW: Stacksteads railway station 1952 — platform view looking towards Bacup. (BL).

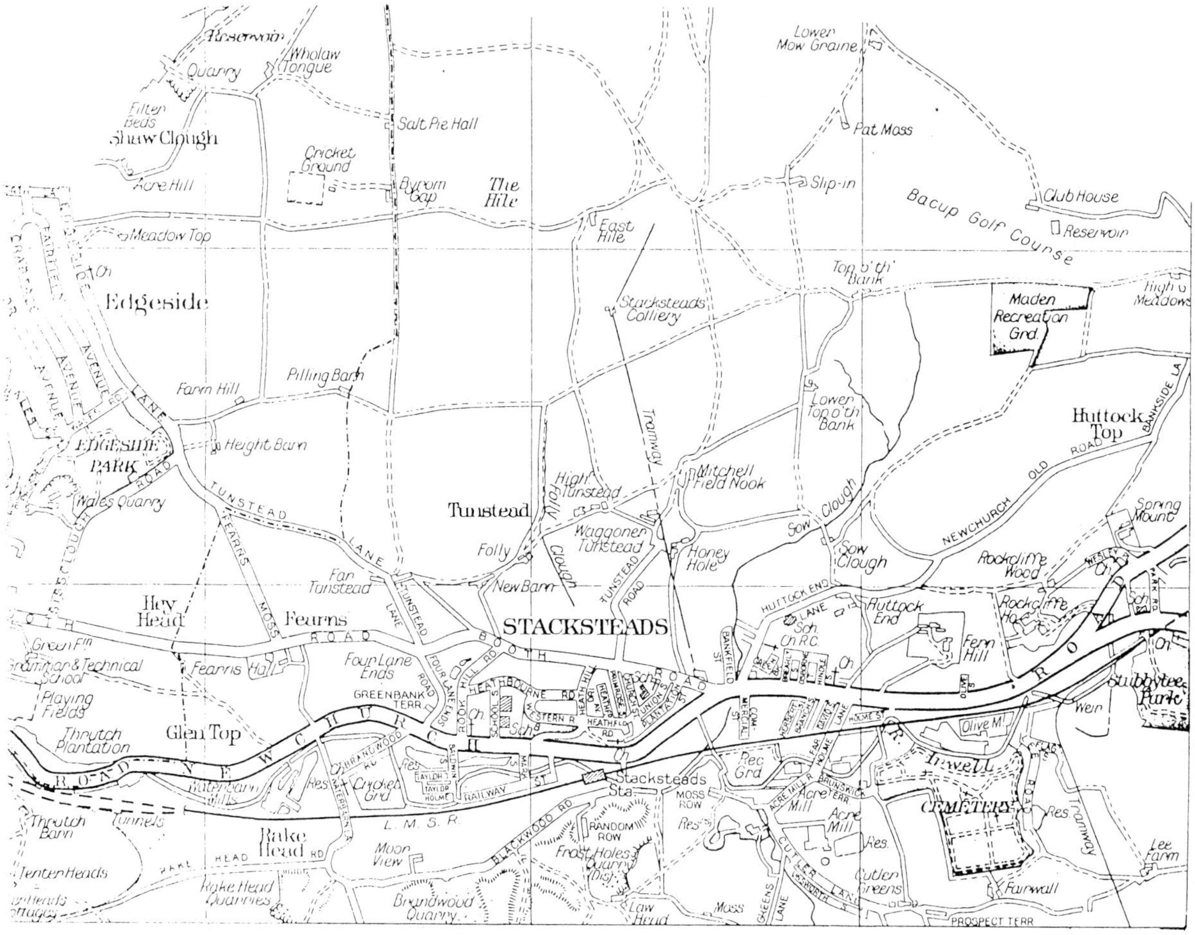

Reservoir
Quarry
Wholaw Tongue
Filter Beds
Shaw Clough
Salt Pie Hall
Cricket Ground
Acre Hill
Byrom Gap
The Hile
Lower Mow Graine
Pat Moss
Slip-in
Bacup Golf Course
Club House
Reservoir
Meadow Top
East Hile
Top o'th' Bank
Edgeside
Stacksteads Colliery
Maden Recreation Grd.
Farm Hill
Pilling Barn
Lower Top o'th' Bank
Huttock Top
Edgeside Park
Height Barn
Tramway
Mitchell Field Nook
High Tunstead
Wales Quarry
Tunstead Lane
Tunstead
Waggoner Tunstead
Sow Clough
Newchurch Old Road
Spring Mount
Honey Hole
Folly
Clough
Rockcliffe Wood
Fan Tunstead
New Barn
Huttock End
Hey Head
Fearns
Stacksteads
Rockcliffe Ho.
Green Fm
Grammar & Technical School
Fearns Hall
Four Lane Ends
Fern Hill
Playing Fields
Greenbank Terr.
Stubbylee Park
Thrutch Plantation
Glen Top
Newchurch Road
Olive Ml
Weir
Waterbarn Mills
Cricket Grd.
Stacksteads Sta.
Rec Grd
Irwell
Railway St
Moss Row
Acre Mill
Cemetery
Res.
Thrutch Barn
Tunnels
L.M.S.R.
Random Row
Rake Head
Blackwood Rd
Tenter Heads
Rake Head Rd
Moon View
Frost Holes Quarry (Dis.)
Cutler Lane
Cutler Greens
Lee Farm
Rake Head Quarries
Brandwood Quarry
Law Head
Moss
Greens Lane
Fairwall
Prospect Terr

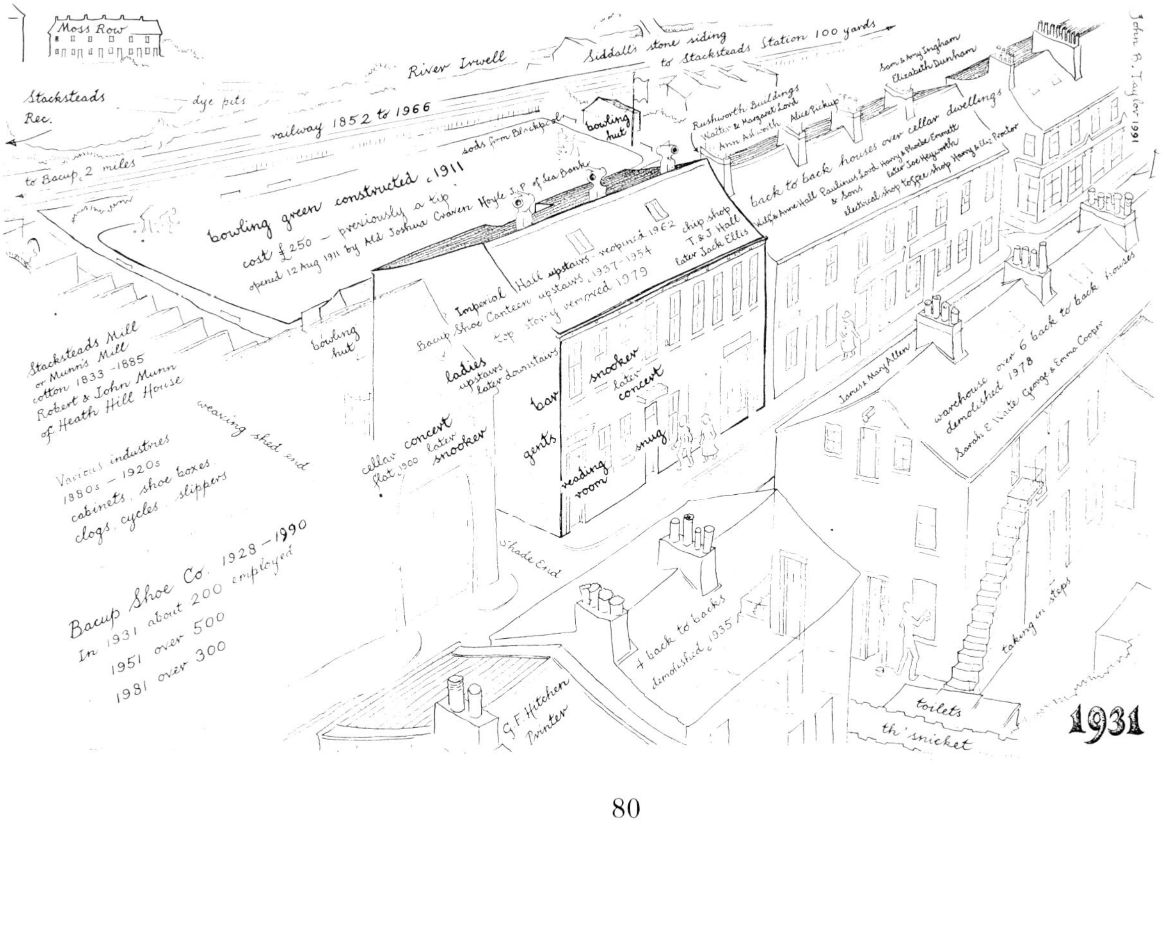

Moss Row
River Irwell
Siddall's stone siding to Stacksteads Station 100 yards
Stacksteads Rec.
dye pits
railway 1852 to 1966
to Bacup 2 miles
sods from Blackpool
bowling hut
bowling green constructed 1911
cost £250 – previously a tip
opened 12 Aug 1911 by Ald Joshua Craven Hoyle J.P. of Lea Bank
Rushworth Buildings
back to back houses over cellar dwellings
chip shop T & J Hall later Jack Ellis
Imperial Hall upstairs reopened 1962
Bacup Shoe Canteen upstairs 1937–1954
top storey removed 1979
bowling hut
Stacksteads Mill or Munn's Mill cotton 1833–1885 Robert & John Munn of Heath Hill House
weaving shed end
ladies upstairs later downstairs
snooker later concert
bar
gents
snug
reading room
cellar concert flat 1900 later snooker
Various industries 1880s – 1920s cabinets, shoe boxes clogs, cycles, slippers
warehouse over 6 back to back houses demolished 1978
Shade End
Bacup Shoe Co. 1928–1990
In 1931 about 200 employed
1951 over 500
1981 over 300
4 back to backs demolished 1935
G.F. Hitchen Printer
taking in steps
toilets
th' snicket
John R. Taylor 1991
1931

OPPOSITE ABOVE: Stacksteads — from a Geographia map of 1935; Heath Hill estate has been developed, but Fern Hill has not. (BL) BELOW: A potted history sketch of the area between Toll Bar and Tunstead Church; the former Working Men's Club is now the Rose 'n' Bowl restaurant. (JBT) ABOVE: Stacksteads Band 1974 were runners-up in their section of the National championships at Bacup Leisure Hall (GC) BELOW: Taylor Holme — a character on the set of *Hindle Wakes*, personally directed by Laurence Olivier in December 1976; across the road is part of Atherton Holme Mill. (BNHS)

ABOVE LEFT: Bacup Borough arms: Honor et Industria, granted 13 March 1883. (BL) RIGHT: Borough of Bacup: common seal 1882. (BL) BELOW LEFT: George Shepherd, JP (1833-1906), one of Bacup's first two county councillors, lived at Holmes Villa, and was the nephew of the owner of Holmes Mill. (BL) RIGHT: Ada Rhodes, MBE (1885-1985), Mayoress of Bacup 1948-9, Mayor 1956-7, Alderman, county councillor, and freeman of Bacup 1959; teacher, organist, and organiser of the local Cancer Research Campaign. (JH)

Those in Control

In 1831 a national cholera epidemic was triggered off by a virulent Asiatic strain which hit Sunderland in the summer and reached Manchester the following spring. This resulted in a meeting on 24 November 1831 convened at the George & Dragon Inn by local magistrate James Whitaker in collaboration with the sole Bacup vicar at the time, Rev William Porter (incumbent of St John's Church for 42 years). The result was the formation of a Board of Health for 'Bacup Booth and Brandwood Higher End as commonly understood to be within the Chapelry of Bacup'.

A medical attendant and inspector were appointed to visit people in their homes and report on the condition of both. Initial investigations revealed 35 cases of sickness, but only one dangerous — a case of putrid typhus. In five days the inspector visited 171 houses, in which 798 people lived.

However, the Board's activities only lasted as long as the cholera scare, for 'the higher the town, the less the cholera mortality rate' appeared to be. So the village of Bacup, with a population assessed in 1831 at about 6,400, was one of many which ignored the Municipal Corporations Act of 1835 and, by missing this initial opportunity to tackle public health, had no effective local government, and no sewerage system.

Edwin Chadwick's influential *Report on the Sanitary Conditions of the Labouring Population* in 1842 was followed by a Royal Commission on the Health of Towns, which resulted in the first Public Health Act of 1848. This set up a General Board of Health, empowered to implement the Act in any place where the local death rate exceeded 23 per 1,000. The Board had five inspectors, one of whom was a civil engineer named William Lee.

There was considerable opposition to the adoption of the 1848 Public Health Act in Bacup, a measure which had no teeth, and in practice Bacup sent *two* deputations to the Board, one in favour of the Act — which resulted in Lee's first visit to Bacup, the other, led by John Bright (MP for Manchester 1847-1852) and John Wilson Patten (Tory MP for Lancashire North) in opposition.

When Lee made his 'preliminary enquiry into the sewerage, drainage and supply of water, and the sanitary condition of the inhabitants of Bacup', mill magnates such as Robert Munn and Thomas Aitken were among those who considered the whole proceedings illegal and invalid, on the grounds that the original petition had not been signed by one tenth of the ratepayers of the chapelry district, so Lee made a further visit and report in April 1850, when some of the witnesses varied their previous statements so much they had clearly been 'got at'. John Holt of Stubbylee advocated a Private Improvement Act (compulsory) rather than the Public Health Act (permissive), but though one was put forward in 1853, nothing came of it.

Disease remained rampant, and infant mortality remained high during the 1850s, until the Parish Church graveyard was more than comfortably full. On 21 June 1858, Dr Worrall chaired the first meeting of the first compulsory representative public body, the Burial Board for the 'Consolidated Chapelry of St John's'. Nearly four years later, the municipal cemetery opened, the first person to be interred being Hannah Howarth (46) of Britannia, who was laid to rest on 12 April 1862.

In December 1863, elections for membership of Bacup Local Board (which Inspector Lee in his naivety had recommended for September 1850) were held, and Dr Worrall headed the poll with 345 votes. Its first chairman was John Dawson, JP for two counties. Meetings of the Local Board were held in the Mechanics' Hall until a Council chamber was built above the shops in the 1867 Market Hall. At the time, the district was divided into five wards: Bacup (which had six members), Greave, Acre Mill, Rockliffe, and Broadclough wards (three representatives each).

In 1863 the population of Bacup was 14,500, living in 3,301 houses, and with a rateable value of £33,055. The general district rate levied in 1864 was 8d in the £, rising to 9d in 1865 and 1s 2d in 1866.

At the time Bacup was divided by the River Irwell from the town centre to Waterfoot, and by the Greave and Sharney brooks running up to the county boundary above Sharneyford. The effect of this was to put Britannia and the southern side of Bacup in the township of Spotland (Hundred of Salford), and the northern side in the Parish of Newchurch-in-Rossendale (Hundred of Blackburn). As the 1832 Reform Bill had divided Lancashire into two parts: a Northern Division, comprising the hundreds of Lonsdale, Amounderness, Leyland and Blackburn, and a Southern Division, including the hundreds of Salford and West Derby, Bacup had a say between 1832 and 1867 in the election of every Lancashire MP — two members being returned for each Division. W. E. Gladstone was MP for Lancashire South from 1865 until constituency boundaries were changed in 1867, when J. M. Holt became the first MP for the new Lancashire North-East constituency in 1868. In June 1885 Rossendale was created a separate constituency, with Bacup the election town, results being declared from the Mechanics' Hall. In November, Lord Hartington was elected as Rossendale's first MP. The Rossendale constituency remained basically unchanged until 1948, when the urban district of Ramsbottom was added, with Whitworth added in 1971 and Darwen in 1983 — which latter had belonged to the ancient Forest of Rossendale centuries before.

Meanwhile, Bacup's Burial Board amalgamated with the Local Board of Health in 1881, and in 1882 the rates for the district (which since 1876 had been extended to take in Stacksteads, Waterbarn and part of Cowpe, a total of 4,800 acres and about 6,400 people) had reached 2s 8d in the £, compared with 2s in 1880 and 2s 4d in 1881. A contributory factor to the increase was the added responsibility for roads caused by the ending of the turnpike trusts.

On 22 August 1882, Bacup was incorporated as a municipal borough, the first of the Rossendale Valley towns to achieve this status, and the most elevated municipal borough in the country. Elections for the new Town Council resulted in 24 councillors, six of whom were elected the first Aldermen of Bacup, necessitating bye-elections for six further councillors. The last meeting of the old Bacup Local Board took place on 30 October 1882, and the first meeting of Bacup Borough Council ten days later.

The Charter of Incorporation delineated six Wards — Brandwood, Tong, Greave, Broadclough, Tunstead and Irwell, each of whom returned one alderman and three councillors. The arms were granted on 13 March 1883, together with the civic motto HONOR ET INDUSTRIA. The (busy) bees in the coat of arms referred to the thrifty and hard-working people, or to industry in general, as well as standing for the initial letter of Bacup, while the two gold bales of cotton, the black fleece or sheepskin, and the block of stone represented specific principal industries. The squirrel and the stag surmounting the arms symbolised the former Forest of Rossendale.

The first of Bacup's 17 town clerks was James Heyworth, previously clerk to the Local Board, who died at the age of only 53 on 9 April 1894. The first chief citizen was Alderman James Hargreaves, who after two years was succeeded as Mayor by Dr William James Clegg, and in 1886 by James Smith Sutcliffe, donor in February 1885 of the mayoral chain.

By that time the number of burgesses on the electoral roll, *ie* eligible to vote, had reached 4,619 out of a total population of over 25,000. Meetings of the Council and its committees, like those of the Local Board before it, took place in a room above the Market Hall. This was considered inappropriate on a long term basis, and in July 1893 the question arose of building new municipal buildings at Hempsteads, a move approved by 13 votes to 4. The architects were told to keep building costs to £10,000, and quoted £9,997 for premises with a 93-foot high clock tower, but the scheme was never implemented, and the Crown post office later occupied part of the intended site.

In 1894 Bacup's boundaries were rationalised by the transfer of the relevant portion of Spotland from the Rochdale Union to the Haslingden one, while the parts of Newchurch and Spotland townships now matched the official municipal boundaries of Bacup.

The Borough acquired a police force in 1887, and a fire brigade in 1893. But there were still complaints about the River Irwell — 'an infernal, virulent, arrant sewer', according to the *Bacup Times*, and the water supply was still inadequate.

At a similar time new sewerage works were proposed for Glen Top, but the Local Government Board did not feel there was enough room at the Thrutch for the filter-beds, so a joint scheme for the three Rossendale townships at Ewood Bridge went ahead.

Meanwhile, the vehicle which continued its nightly round of emptying all the pail closets in town gave rise to the *Song of the Corporation muck cart*, which was apparently sung by lads coming from the pits in the hearing of lasses going to the mills at 5.30 am:

The corporation Muck Cart was full up to the brim,
The driver fell inside it and found he couldn't swim;
He sank to the bottom just like a little stone,
And then they heard him singing that 'There's no place like home'.

Eventually, after a meeting of local ratepayers in 1919 approved the conversion of Stubbylee Hall into a town hall, the borough council moved all its activities there, apart from the rates office (Market Street), health department (until 1947), and electricity department (until 1 April 1948).

The Council chamber at Stubbylee Hall was first used on 9 November 1920, and until 1974 Bacup operated its municipal services from Stubbylee, where the Council resolved 'that the purchase of all newspapers except one copy of the Manchester Guardian for the Town Clerk per day, and of the "Justice of the Peace" for use of the officials be discontinued'. Council departments achieved an enviable reputation for efficiency — especially in relation to snow-clearing. Whenever wintry weather hit Bacup, it usually took less than an hour for the gritters to salt and grit the roads quickly and efficiently.

Under the Local Government Act 1888 and the County Electors Act 1888 Bacup was assigned two divisions on the original Lancashire County Council: (a) the North-West division, comprising Broadclough, Irwell and Tunstead wards; and (b) the South-East division, comprising Greens, Tong and Brandwood wards — with the local waterways again forming the boundary between them.

Bacup's first county councillors, George Shepherd (of Holmes Villa) and Henry Maden, were returned unopposed in January 1889, and in the immediate election for county aldermen, Henry Maden topped the poll. Just three Bacup men have been county aldermen: Henry Maden, James Shuttleworth (who became the second Chairman of the county's main roads and bridges committee, 1907-1913), and Henry Heys (1928-1933). Until 1936 Bacup had two representatives at County Hall, but during the life of the 1889-1974 Lancashire County Council, twenty different councillors represented Bacup's interests.

After the Great War, women were granted the vote, became eligible for election as MPs and other public offices. As a result, Mrs Zipporah Mountain was appointed Bacup's first lady magistrate in March 1920. She died at the end of 1927.

During its lifetime, Bacup has granted the Freedom of the Borough to 16 people, including Walter Nuttall, last survivor of the original Irwell Springs Band, and Ada Rhodes, 'Mrs Bacup', one of only two women to be Mayor of Bacup, and the sole councillor to be both Mayoress and later Mayor in her own right, as well as an Alderman of Bacup Council and a Lancashire County Councillor for four years.

In 1969, the Redcliffe-Maud report on the future of local government proposed that Bacup, together with Rawtenstall, should go into an enlarged Burnley district — a recommendation which cut no ice with the government. A new commission in 1972 opted for a huge new authority combining Rossendale and Accrington, and stretching from Whitworth to Great Harwood but, after a public inquiry, a Rossendale unitary authority was set up as the 14th district of a truncated Lancashire County.

So on 1 April 1974, Bacup Borough, with a total rateable value for 1973-74 of £834,326, a population of 14,990, and rates of 32p in the £, became part of a united Rossendale Borough, whose council included twelve councillors from Rawtenstall, nine from each of Bacup and Haslingden, four from Whitworth, two from Edenfield and two from Stubbins, making a total of 38. In 1974-75 Bacup's proportion of the Rossendale rates was 54.31p in the £, and 66.65p the following year.

Elections for the new Rossendale Council resulted in three members being returned for each of three Bacup wards: 1 (Farholme and Waterbarn), 2 (Broadclough and Greens), 3 (Irwell and Tong). Ward 1, the eastern ward, is now Stacksteads; Ward 2, the eastern ward, has become Greensclough; and Ward 3 is simply the Irwell ward.

Stubbylee Hall is still in use. In April 1974 it housed the Leisure and Recreation department; now the whole of the Engineering and Planning department operates from there. A Council presence is maintained in the town centre by the Bacup Neighbourhood Office, operative from 1986.

James Heyworth (1841-1894), clerk to Bacup local board, first town clerk of Bacup Borough (1882-94) and one of the teachers at Bacup Ragged School.
(BL)

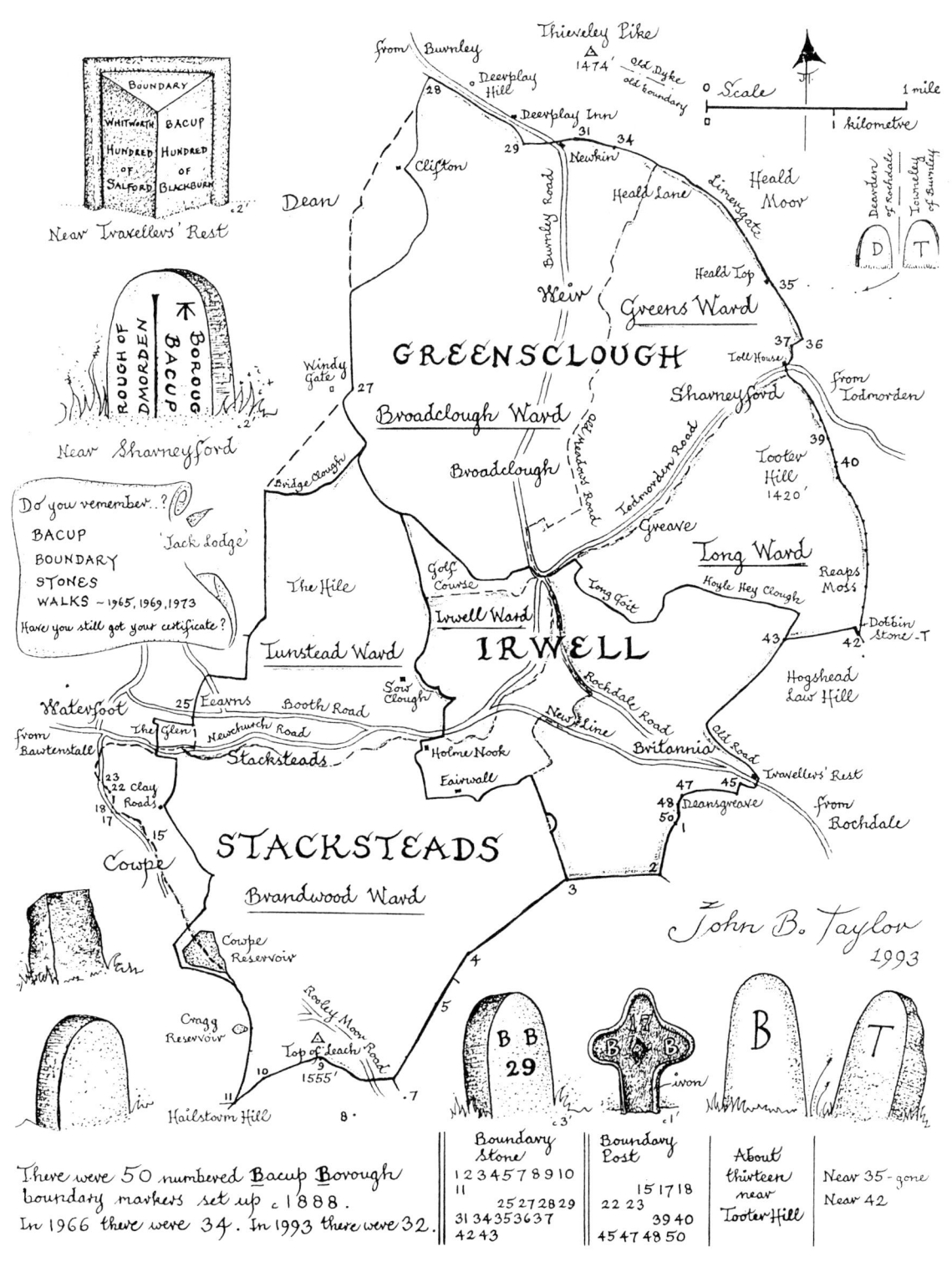

Bacup's boundaries — showing the three main wards (named in capitals), the former wards of Bacup Borough (underlined), and indicating the whereabouts of extant boundary stones and posts. (JBT)

LEFT: Lawrence Heyworth (1786-1872), Bacup entrepreneur, businessman, Chairman of the Mechanics' Institute 1841-1872 and father of four children was grandfather to Beatrice Webb (née Potter), and great-grandfather to Sir Stafford Cripps, Richard Durning Holt (Liberal candidate for Rossendale in the 1922 General Election), and Kitty Dobbs, who in 1927 married Malcolm Muggeridge. RIGHT: Bacup School Board: Certificate of Merit for 1898. Joshua Thomas Hoyle (1858-1937), Board Chairman, was the only Mayor of Bacup not a member of the Council at the time (1920-23), and initiated the Central Aid Fund. BELOW: Mechanics' Hall, Bacup, c1960, showing the corn mill behind. (HO'N)

In Pursuit of Learning

The old chapel or school-house in Bacup Fold was used mainly for religious purposes for most of the 18th century, though some education took place as well. After the death of Joseph Booth at the early age of 41 in 1819, James Maden of Greens, a trustee, was responsible for appointing a kinsman, James Taylor, a descendant of the Whitworth Doctors, as the new schoolmaster, with the proviso that the schoolroom should be kept free 'for the use of the Sunday scholars on the Sabbath day'.

The 1802 Health and Morals of Apprentices Act required the three Rs to be taught according to age and ability 'in some room set apart for that purpose', and resulted in a few early private schools. The most significant was one which met, by courtesy of the Munn brothers, in a room above the boiler at Irwell Mill. This was Clegg's Academy, which ceased after the premature death of Roger Clegg in 1840.

Bacup Mechanics' Institute set out to provide education for working people with no other opportunity for improving themselves, opening in rented premises on New Year's Day 1840, providing the first library and the first museum in Bacup. Members keeping books a week overdue in 1844 were to be fined 1½d, and 3d per week after that.

The Institution held an annual general meeting and soirée (or tea party), early ones being held elsewhere because their own rented premises were not big enough. In 1846, needing to expand, the present Mechanics' Hall was built at a cost of £1,300 on the site of the oldest nonconformist place of worship in Rossendale. Local businessman Lawrence Heyworth of Greensnook succeeded Robert Munn as President in January 1841, and remained President until his death on 19 April 1872, when the Institute went into mourning for three months.

This non-denominational day-school was something unique at a time when all other schools were church-related, and became the major independent educational establishment in Bacup. By 1855 the day school was catering for 40 day scholars plus 176 mill children. The number of day scholars (130) exceeded the number of factory children (122) in 1861, when one subject taught was decimal coinage . . .

Robert Stewart, pupil teacher in 1863 and assistant master 1864, became at the age of 23 in 1868 master of both day and evening schools. He took over a day school with 248 children on the books, and an evening school with an average attendance of 167. The day-school average attendance peaked at 312 in 1879, though the evening classes had peaked five years earlier at 194. In 1883, 95% of his pupils passed the 3 Rs examinations. He resigned in July 1891.

Meanwhile, Robert Raikes of Gloucester had pioneered popular education, in particular the Sunday School movement. Many people however thought that to allow boys and girls to reach the age of 11 or over without having learned a trade would lead to their ruin. The question of literacy did not appear to matter. It is estimated that in 1800 in England and Wales, one out of three males were illiterate and a higher proportion of females.

A few years later, Joseph Lancaster initiated his school in London — the beginning of voluntary supported day schools. In 1814 this became known as the British and Foreign School Society, better known as British Schools, nonconformist in origin. The use of slates in schools stemmed from his discovery that slates from demolished houses made good writing surfaces.

Not to be outdone, the then Archbishop of Canterbury initiated in October 1811 the 'National Society for the Education of the Poor, throughout England and Wales, in the Principles of the Established Church', which became known as National Schools.

Reading, writing and arithmetic were all included in the curricula of both National and British schools, though the standards reached were somewhat limited.

22-year-old Enoch Priestley (1818-1891) and his brother John taught at a night-school established at Heald for young people whose early employment in the mills left them little time for learning. He earned a reputation for teaching girls and boys to knit and sew as well as to read and write. In 1842 when the day schoolmaster died, Enoch Priestley was appointed in his place without any guaranteed salary, and subsequently taught at Sharneyford as an uncertificated teacher.

Bacup's first National school was built in 1828, primarily to serve St John's Church as a Sunday School, and after the June 1831 exams, scholars were rewarded with buns and spiced ale.

When Edward Baines investigated the social, educational and religious state of the manufacturing districts in 1843, he found Bacup the least literate area in Rossendale — a mere 50% of the 3,862 scholars in Bacup Sunday Schools were able to read. However, Bacup Primitive Methodists took literacy seriously, and from 1842 to 1854 used a room in Market Street as a weekday school. At one stage they even dispensed with their Sunday morning worship service so that more time could be given to the teaching of writing.

At that time, the most to which the poorest children could aspire was the ability to sign their name(s) — the strict interpretation of 'literacy' — and to read a little. But the rapid rise in elementary education meant that by 1870 four adults in five were literate and, by the end of the century, illiteracy in England had been virtually eliminated.

Most Bacup children were sent to work as early as possible for economic reasons. Their labour represented an important part of the family budget. But the 1833 Factory Act contained a proviso that from 1836 no children below the age of nine should be employed in mills or factories, while those between the ages of nine and 13 should have attended school for at least two hours a day.

This proved a springboard for educational activity. The number of schools in Bacup doubled by 1838, and educational facilities were provided at ten different schools by 1870. One private school in New Line, when only half-a-dozen houses existed, was capably run by David Bolton, who had lost an arm in an accident at Waterbarn Mill when he was only 11 years old, but who was Weir's oldest man when he died at the age of 92 in January 1915.

The system under which working-class children divided their day between school and factory became known as the half-time system. In 1870, St Mary's School had the highest proportion of half-timers: 80 out of 85 girls attended the day-school, and 70 out of 120 day boys. At Mount Pleasant Wesleyans, 115 out of 135 boys and 121 out of 195 girls were half-timers. In 1879 about 40% of the child population in the Newchurch School Board area were half-timers, and by 1892 Lancashire had the highest number of half-timers in the country — 93,969, the Bacup proportion being 1,694 (833 boys and 861 girls). In 1893 the minimum age for part-time employment was raised to 11, and to 12 in 1899 — despite the Mayor's view that as 11-year-olds were so happy at their work, why deprive them of it for another year? Half-time employment was finally abolished by the 1918 Education Act.

Under Forster's Elementary Education Act of 1870, each of the nine parishes or townships in Rossendale became school districts. There were enough school places in the Newchurch district to accommodate all the pupils in the area, including Sharneyford, but the Education Department felt that Sharneyford needed a school of its own. Eventually premises were rented from the Wesleyans until a new school could be built and opened in March 1878 at a total cost of £3,387 15s 4d. When the mill at Sharneyford closed, the school built to accommodate 200 was left with an average attendance of 65, and it has never reached 100 since.

The Revised Code of 1862 introduced payment by results. Head teachers' income was geared to the government grant, the size of which depended, not only on the number of children on roll, but the actual attendances of those children, 50% being the minimum permissible. This system discriminated against schools in working-class area where there were many half-timers. However, in November 1883, seven-year-old Emma Jane Hargreaves died from 'inflammation of the brain caused by overwork at school'. The case merited a leader column in the *Bacup Times*, and was also reported in the national press. The immediate result was the stopping of 'home lessons' for very young children. The medical authorities tended to blame the Education Act 'with its present system of payment by results' . . . or what was even then called 'the cramming system'.

Children in upper standards were often grouped together in higher grade schools catering especially for them, though none were set up by Bacup School Board (formed August 1883). Mount Pleasant Day School was large enough to warrant a higher grade *class*, and in 1886 John F. Wilkinson, formerly at Newchurch Grammar School, established a Higher Grade School which ran for nine years until 1895.

Bacup School Board initiated a scheme for religious instruction, beginning each day with the Lord's Prayer or a hymn, a daily Bible reading (without note or comment), and a vesper. Once a week the Ten Commandments were to be recited.

School attendance was affected by haymaking in the summer, when farmers' children inevitably helped; heavy winter snowfalls; local epidemics and school fees, 25% of Tunstead scholars depending on charity for their school fees/pence in January 1864. School attendance was only made compulsory in 1876, when the onus for attendance was placed on the parent who was liable to a fine of 5s otherwise. In 1891 education at last became free, and the Assisted Education Act of 1891 led to wholesale changes in local schools, including adequate toilet accommodation, cloakroom space and classroom area — as well as proper and separate provision for infants.

In January 1867 a British School had been opened at Doals. It had no connection with either the church or the Sunday school, but was managed by a separate committee of managers. By 1890 it was finding things financially difficult, and after one refusal by Bacup School Board to accept responsibility for it, it was taken over by them in 1892. Heald Wesleyan School promptly followed suit.

The provision of technical education was another desirable improvement, but by 1886 neither the income nor the premises of the Mechanics' Institute were adequate to cope with any extras. Eventually in 1892, James Hargreaves, President of the Mechanics' Institute, rented his Spring Gardens Mill in Tong Lane at a nominal rent of £20 per annum for use as a technical school. Control of the Mechanics' Institute passed to Bacup School Board until it ceased as a place of learning at the end of 1908. A Mechanics' Institute Scholarship fund still enables students between the ages of 18 and 25 to pursue a course of study after at least one year working in a relevant industry.

In August 1893, Waterbarn managers offered their British School to the Board, and Stacksteads Wesleyans abolished their school fees to prevent a mass exodus to Waterbarn.

In June 1897 the Wesleyan school was taken over by the School Board, the schools inspector envisaging Stacksteads being run as an infants school, and Waterbarn as a mixed school for older children. Unfortunately, reports on both premises highlighted adverse factors. Consequently, Western School, opened in April 1903, was built to accommodate 600 boys and girls and 300 infants at a cost of £15,969 14s.

Britannia Wesleyan School was taken over by Bacup School Board in 1893, and in June 1901 the managers of Mount Pleasant offered their school to the Board, who six months later took it over on a 30-year lease. As the infants' department was not considered satisfactory, the children were temporarily housed at Mount Olivet Sunday School up Lanehead until Mount Infants Council School was opened in July 1905.

A site at Thorn Meadows, 880 feet above sea-level, was bought to replace the school at the Mechanics' Institute. The infants department, accommodating 325, opened in September 1895, and the mixed department a year later with places for another 504. The final cost of these new Central Schools was £19,983.

At Weir, the Education Department wanted a new school by June 1896 to replace two unsatisfactory sets of premises, but Bacup School Board demurred, feeling that if local mills closed, as they had up Sharneyford, and the population decreased as a result, they probably would not need a new school. In practice, it took 14 years for a site to be agreed and eventually Northern School was finished, 998½ feet above sea-level, and officially opened on 13 August 1910 at a cost of £6,000 for the building and £1,120 for the site, 17 years after Heald School had first been condemned by the Education Department.

During 1904 Bacup Education Committee (which had taken over from Bacup School Board following the 1902 Education Act) was contemplating taking over Wesley Place and St Saviour's schools, using one for infants and the other for seniors, but in September the Board of Education condemned Wesley Place. St Saviour's had only two teachers when they ought to have had five so, after some hard bargaining, St Saviour's day school was leased to the local education authority as a county primary school for 406 boys and girls, while the Board of Education recognised Wesley Place for 204 infants. The latter lasted until the end of March 1925 when pupils transferred to St Saviour's. By that time the number of school places in Bacup was recorded as 4,862, a figure which dropped to 4,658 in February 1926, to 4,512 in October 1928, and rose to 4,592 in June 1939.

In February 1905, all the half-timers were removed from Mount (Pleasant) and sent to the Central School, a successful effort to make a full class of half-time pupils. The next move was to bring together all the half-timers in Bacup (234 at the time) at one school. Mount Pleasant, shorn of its half-timers, continued until July 1939, by which time a new senior school had been opened at Blackthorn at a cost of £45,000, with a capacity of 480. When it opened, 171 scholars and six members of staff transferred from Central Junior School, thus concluding a period of 14 years known as the 'selective era', when pupils between the ages of 11 and 14 had been transferred from other junior schools in Bacup.

During the Bacup School Board era, prospective teachers could become pupil teachers at the age of 14. Their day extended beyond the normal school day of 9 am to 5 pm, with an hour's tuition from their head teacher from 5.30 to 6.30 pm — an hour eventually transferred to the early morning from 7.45 to 8.45 am before school began. In addition, they were expected to attend night school twice a week.

After the completion of their 'apprenticeship' three years later, success in a 'Queen's Scholarship' examination would entitle a pupil teacher to train at a teacher training college — but few places were available. A local Pupil Teachers' Centre was needed. One began at Accrington in 1897, but Bacup had to wait until 1904, when one opened in Bethel School at Waterfoot. This amalgamated in 1913 with the old Newchurch Grammar School to form Bacup and Rawtenstall Joint Secondary School, for entry to which scholarship examinations were introduced — the 11+.

During the pupil-teacher centre years, girls from Bacup had to attend the Bacup Technical School premises in Spring Gardens for lessons in art and chemistry. The Joint Secondary School was renamed Bacup and Rawtenstall Grammar School in 1928.

The education of Bacup Catholic children began for St Joseph's in premises adjoining Wesley Place, but eventually a new school-chapel was built in 1892, a move approved both by the Bishop of Salford and by the Department of Education. St Mary's opened a school in 1872 adjacent to the church, followed by enlarged premises in Dale Street in 1904, but in 1956 they were declared inadequate and unsafe; as a temporary expedient scholars were housed in the former Bacup Liberal Club until their new school virtually on the moors was opened in October 1959.

By 1938, a new mixed senior Catholic school was being mooted to serve Bacup's two parishes. However, the war precluded any activity, and in 1944 the Butler Education Act made the provision of some form of secondary education mandatory, the school-leaving age having been raised to 15 from September 1939. (It would rise to 16 in 1972). Bacup already had a senior school at Blackthorn, but this needed to be supplemented. For the Catholics, a suitable property was found in Rawtenstall at Brynbella, formerly the home of Miss Caroline Whitehead, who died on 22 September 1945. Here, St Ambrose Secondary School, built to satisfy the requirements of the 1944 Education Act, opened in 1960 with 450 pupils, 150 from the Bacup area, and was renamed All Saints in September 1978.

Fearns School began in the mid-1950s as a couple of classes in part of Western primary school. As it expanded — five classes and seven teachers in 1957 — expeditions to St Joseph's (for woodwork) and Thorn (for domestic science) were necessary before premises at Fearns Moss were built astride the official boundary between Bacup and Rawtenstall, and serving both towns. It was officially opened in November 1959, and further extensions were scheduled to accommodate more pupils, and would ultimately lead to the closure of Blackthorn, which ceased in the summer of 1985. Fearns took the title of High School in January 1991.

In April 1940, Central School was renamed Thorn, running infant and junior schools until the summer of 1982, when it became known as Thorn County Primary School, absorbing pupils from Mount Infants School at the end of 1982. Four years later, when the premises were condemned, the school was transferred to the former Blackthorn buildings with effect from September 1986, and remains the largest primary school in Bacup.

An adverse report on St Saviour's school in 1949 was followed by a devastating one early in 1982, which led to the immediate vacation and demolition of the premises. Eventually, in June 1983, the school returned to temporary accommodation on the Church Meadow part of Stubbylee Park. Western and Tunstead schools merged as Holy Trinity, Stacksteads, which was officially opened on the site of the former coal staithe on 4 July 1987.

Over the years the number of children at Bacup's schools has varied considerably: 2,761 in 1875, 3,523 in 1879, 2,998 in 1913, 2,877 on roll in 1932, 1,395 on roll in January 1987, and 1,204 at the beginning of the 1993-94 school year.

Many factors have contributed to Bacup's educational history, varying from small dame schools run by unknown individuals to the night-school classes run by the Mechanics' Institutes and other schools, and the Workers' Educational Association, which began in Bacup in 1931, and was visited in February 1939 by Archbishop William Temple of York who spoke on the 'Secret of Freedom'.

At least the 'savage ignorance' on which a Government inspector of schools felt obliged to comment in June 1849 is no longer prevalent.

ABOVE: Central Board Schools 1906, Infant and Junior buildings, were demolished in 1987 and replaced by a cluster of modern bungalows named Central View. BELOW: Fearns School (c1960) has since been extended.

War and Hard Times

July 1913 saw the only Royal visit in the history of Rossendale. As part of a public relations exercise at a time of rising prices, George V and Queen Mary embarked on an unofficial week-long 'industrial tour' of Lancashire, and on Wednesday, 9 July, they visited eight industrial towns, Bacup being the seventh on the list.

Mills and workshops in Bacup closed at noon, sub-post offices closed at 1 pm, and one enterprising shopkeeper had his upstairs window cleaned for the first time since Queen Victoria's Diamond Jubilee in 1897. Christ Church bell ringers rang a royal bon of 720 peals.

Stacksteads Band struck up the *National Anthem* as the Daimler flying the Royal Standard passed Heath Hill, and at precisely 4.42 pm the Royal car hove into sight at Sandfield, where some 3,500 schoolchildren were assembled. Their Majesties' stay in Bacup lasted precisely eight minutes, where they were the first couple to sign the Borough's newly-acquired visitors' book, before travelling on down the Whitworth Valley.

When war broke out a year later, the symbol of military recruitment was still the King's Shilling, a rate unchanged for over a century. Bacup generally shared the national atmosphere of patriotism and confidence in early victory.

Munitions works were introduced at Irwell Mill, where 4.5 inch shell cases were produced, and steel filings (swarf) collected for re-use. Height Barn Mill also became a shell factory. A Bacup contingent of St John Ambulance volunteers was the first batch of sick berth reservists to report for duty; Fern Hill House was requisitioned as a convalescent home for the wounded; a Defence Corps was mobilised at Stacksteads and a civilian corps at Bacup.

The Bacup War Comforts Association was active; a Special Constabulary was formed to help to maintain local law and order and the local military tribunal deployed non-combatant males to useful areas of 'national service'.

The war had a direct effect on every day life. Male labour forces were decimated, and women had to fill the gaps. Many commodities were in short supply: cotton, for instance, and coal; coal dust, or tiny bits of coal, which normally would be thrown away, were made into briquettes, about the size of a duck's egg. When food shortages became acute, butter was eked out by boiling and mashing potatoes and mixing the butter in. The cultivation of smallholdings and school gardens was encouraged.

Shortages in all materials demanded extra resourcefulness, so when the gnarled old ash tree which gave its name to Ash Street fell with an almighty crash one windy night, the smaller branches were used as fuel — in short supply anyway — and the trunk was cut up by a local clogger and used later in the manufacture of clog soles.

Rationing came late. 'Voluntary rationing' was emphasised, and the nation asked to confine itself to 4 lbs of bread, 2½ lbs of meat and ¾ lb of sugar per person per week. Most working classes in Bacup couldn't afford anything like that amount of meat, and the bread ration was far too small. Local grocers fell foul of Food Orders of which they claimed ignorance.

A breach of the Oats & Maize Order in 1917 resulted in a fine of 20s plus costs for selling one pound of meal at 5½d instead of 5d. Another grocer was fined a similar amount for charging ⅜d more than he should have done for a quantity of flour. Eventually compulsory rationing restricted sugar from New Year's Day 1918, followed by meat, butter and margarine on April Fool's Day. Food rationing, in gradually modified form, continued until the end of November 1920.

The wartime inflation rate meant that by November 1918, food prices were 133% above the August 1914 level, and the cost of living had more than doubled. Locally it meant that the price of what had been halfpenny bars of chocolate had risen to 2d.

When hostilities ceased, at 11 am on the 11th day of the 11th month, mill hooters sounded, bonfires were lit on Bacup market ground, Stacksteads recreation ground and, after the peace treaty of June 1919, there was another celebratory bonfire on the hills behind Stubbylee.

On Tuesday, 22 July, old folks aged 65 or more were given a treat — tea at the Co-operative Hall, followed by entertainment at the Mechanics' Hall. Stacksteads guests were similarly treated and entertained at Waterbarn schoolroom.

In all 515 men of Bacup had given their lives in the Great War of 1914-18, and are commemorated by three tablets now housed in the Aged, Blind & Disabled (AB & D) Centre. For some years thereafter the Mayor of Bacup attended an annual Armistice Day service on 11 November. On 10 November 1928, the Bacup war memorial was unveiled in Hempsteads Gardens.

On the postwar industrial front, the proprietors of Irwell Mill agreed in June 1920 to take 5% of the disabled ex-servicemen on to their workforce.

The 48-hour working week resulted from a three-week strike by cotton operatives in 1919, and as a result the irritating and unpopular pre-breakfast start was terminated. A 7.45 am start was followed by an hour for lunch, and a 5.30 pm finish during the week, and at noon on Saturdays.

However, quarrymen returning from the wars were dismayed to find they were being paid less than a teenage cotton operative. Strikes in the mining and quarrying industries were met by refusals to increase pay; miners' wages were in fact cut three times, leading to the General Strike of May 1926, called in support of miners locked out for not accepting longer hours and lower pay. For nine days there were no trams, no trains, no newspapers, and anyone who ventured to work either walked or went by bicycle. One enterprising farmer supplied one mill with coal from old mine-workings on his land, thus enabling it to keep going through the coal strike.

The Central Aid Fund was instituted by J. T. Hoyle in February 1922 to assist poor and needy local people. Between the wars it dealt with over a hundred applications every year, while the Bacup Borough Hospital Trust Council was set up to help people who could not afford medical care and, if necessary, provide transport to hospital.

A short-lived postwar boom, when prices soared, was followed by a biting slump which caused widespread distress and mass unemployment. In Bacup it reached 28.3% in 1931. The hated Means Test was imposed and unemployment in Lancashire more than doubled between 1929 and 1931. Unemployment in the Lancashire cotton trade rose from 39,153 in October 1937 to 88,164 six months later; Bacup's 15.6% in 1937 rose by a third to 20.7% in 1938.

Industry diversified. Many former cotton mills became shoe factories. John Maden & Son switched to lingerie manufacture and the making of hospital wear. By July 1933 more Bacup workers were employed in the shoe and slipper trade (2,884) than in the cotton industry (2,675), though 22.7% were unemployed.

The Knights of St Columba, active in Bacup for some 60 years, began to relieve cases of distress, in line with the Biblical injunction (James 1 v.27), based on their three virtues of charity, unity, and fraternity.

Local entrepreneur John Willie Johnson set up as a slipper factor in 1936, buying up bankrupt stocks and machinery for which licences were still valid, and found Bacup people diligent in business and able to produce shoes at a price people could afford. By 1939 40% of Bacup people were employed in the footwear industry, as opposed to 30% in the cotton trade, which now had only twelve mills left in Bacup.

Then on 3 September came the Prime Minister's announcement that 'This country is at war with Germany . . .' Bacup people went about in their usual phlegmatic fashion. Trenches had been dug, gas masks distributed, air raid shelters constructed at three different sites, and four lock-up shops under the Market Hall sandbagged for emergency use. If a gas attack should be imminent, hand-*rattles* would sound — and when the danger was over, hand-*bells* would sound.

Shops (except for newsagents and tobacconists) were obliged to close at 7 pm from the end of October 1939, except for one late night to 8 pm. Street lighting was extinguished, and blackout regulations enforced. If any light(s) showed, air raid wardens would come round shouting 'Put that light out!' Five Bacupians fell foul of the blackout regulations during the first month of the war and were duly summonsed. And the Bacup Brick & Tile Company was fined for showing a glare from their brick kiln at Flowers Mill. Coal rationing was introduced from 1 October 1939.

Children from areas considered at high risk were evacuated — some of them to Bacup. Evacuation was a vexed question. Winston Churchill was opposed to compulsory evacuation, although he was worried about safety if people decided to stay put. In the event, on 24 August came instructions to implement contingency plans made the previous February. Eight days later, and two days before war was actually declared, 223 children from three Manchester schools arrived in Bacup, some of them having got off to an exciting start when their 'bus attempted to go under a bridge too low *en route* for Victoria station.

One was the historian Joyce Marlow who, as a girl of nine, was billeted in Stacksteads with her best friend. There were some hopeless mis-matches: 'some guardians considering the small sums paid by the Government . . . insufficient recompense for the unruly, ungrateful, or homesick kids dumped upon them, and some children utterly miserable in their new houses. One was billeted in a row of small cottages half-way up a Stacksteads hillside. Her hosts may have been the salt of the earth, but the lack of amenities, notably the outside lavatories further up the hillside, sent the little girl, who was rather a spoiled brat, into hysterics'. (Local householders were officially allowed 10s 6d per week for the first child and 8s 6d per week for each additional youngster, though Joyce's guardians only received 8s 6d per child).

Education was shared at local schools on a shift system — evacuees attending Bacup & Rawtenstall Grammar School had the morning shift beginning at 8.30 am while those attending schools in Bacup went from 1 until 5.30 pm, locals and evacuees alternating morning or afternoon in alternate weeks.

Joyce Marlow belonged to the former group, who were expected to walk to school, assembling in the early hours 'outside a small shop at the bottom of the hill from Glenborough Avenue. With only glints of lights from the slits of torches to illuminate the road, we sang jolly songs as we tramped along. After several of us had fallen into ruts or tripped over, our teachers produced a thick rope, to which the youngsters were tied, the rest of us clutched!' Eventually the younger children were transferred to Stacksteads Methodist premises to continue their chequered education though, as the months of the 'Phoney War' passed and no bombs fell, some evacuees returned to Manchester — and failed to return. More evacuees were admitted to a Bacup school in the summer of 1944, driven out of the London area by the doodlebug menace.

Some considered evacuation a mistake, as Bacup was on the 'direct route from Hull', and equally likely to be attacked. Two bombs dropped at Thorn on 21 October 1940, merely damaging a few houses. The newspaper report was deliberately vague so as not to give any geographical secrets away to a presumed enemy. Further bombs fell on 3 May 1941. More potential hoodwinking of the enemy involved the screwing of a rectangular board to the 1862 datestone over the Bacup Co-operative Store, covering over the town name. The stone, permanised in the Wall of History, still bears the four holes.

Bacup played its part with its Local Defence Volunteers, popularly known as the Look, Duck and Vanish Brigade, but renamed by the redoubtable Winston Churchill in July 1940 as the Home Guard. Bacup's five companies under the command of Colonel Harry Hoyle prepared to repel any invasion, supported by Stacksteads Band (known as the Home Guards Band during the period), who kept the spirit alive while most younger members were serving with HM Forces, with Holmes Mill as the Home Guard headquarters.

Each division was responsible for watching one of the main roads into Bacup. A division guarded Newkin and Weir; B company Sharneyford; C company Britannia; D company Stacksteads, while Captain Ben Tattersall directed the mobile company. Air-raid sirens helped 'to maintain a viable early warning system when it was most needed'; they played their part in civilian life too, but were eventually removed in 1993.

During the War, Bacup took part in five special savings weeks: War Weapons Week (May 24-31, 1941, raising £242,228); Warship Week (February 21-28, 1942, £136,346); Wings for Victory Week (June 5-12, 1943, £220,340 — nearly double the target); Salute the Soldier Week (June 10-17, 1944, £206,350); Thanksgiving and Safety Week (November 3-10, 1945, £189,890). A further special effort resulted in an aggregate total of £1,001,304.

Warship Week resulted in the adoption of HMS *Amaranthus*, a 'Flower Class Corvette', one of 300 built for medium distance convoy escorts. Built during 1940, she had already become known as the 'Lagos Ferry' due to her versatility and reliability before being assigned to Bacup in mid-1942. Three more commissions ensued before her days ended in the Far East in 1953. For 30 years a small plaque, hand-carved by one of her crew, was displayed on the landing of Stubbylee Hall.

Economies and a salvage drive for the war effort were promoted. Old rags were seen as vital raw materials. 24 old keys would provide enough metal for a hand-grenade, 84 the metal parts for a rifle, and 126 the metal parts for a tommy gun. Paper was another target: housewives were urged to reduce the consumption of paper for lighting fires by half, and thus make more paper available for re-pulping. Each machine gun bullet carried a wad made from waste paper. Waste-paper compressed into salt-resistant board could catapult aircraft from battleships. And in October 1942, the lattice girder bridge which had spanned Burnley Road at Old Meadows was demolished and used as scrap for the war effort. It had been a Bacup landmark for 47 years, though it had fallen into disuse during the 1930s. Many of the iron railings around churches, schools and private houses were also commandeered for the war effort. £750 worth of waste materials was salvaged in Bacup in 1941-42.

Another advert suggested that 'if everyone took one cup of tea less each day, it would save enough gas in a month to make 69,200 bombs' — energy saving with a vengeance! In practice, it was estimated that by that autumn, Britain was producing more war material per thousand population than any other nation on earth. Patriotic gardening was again encouraged, under the guise of 'Dig for Victory'.

The War Comforts Committee was busy, with Jack Storey's Concert Party raising well over £1,000 for the war effort; and every Saturday, girls would use leg tan if real stockings were unobtainable. Mount Pleasant ran a monthly magazine: *Greetings from t' Top o' t' Brow*, which ran for 63 issues from August 1940 until the end of the war. The saving of bun pennies and ship halfpennies for the Comforts Funds was also encouraged.

Through their work with old people during air raids, the Women's Voluntary Service realised that many elderly people were not being properly nourished on individual wartime rations, typically noted as 3 oz tea, 7 oz fats, 8 oz sugar, ½ lb meat, 3 oz bacon, 4 oz cheese, two eggs, and 2½ pints of milk per week. Sweets and chocolates were rationed from 27 July 1942, and ration books were used for other commodities. This led to the opening of British Restaurants throughout the country. 19 January 1943 marked the opening of Bacup's first British Restaurant and Cooking Centre at Irwell Terrace schoolroom, followed by a second centre at Acre Mill Baptist school in April. Women joining the Civil Defence began taking meals from the British Restaurants to the housebound — the precursor of the present Meals on Wheels service.

The Citizens' Advice Bureau originally opened in Bacup on 6 April 1940, and performed a useful service throughout the war years.

The 1943 Wings for Victory week resulted in Bacup sponsoring a four-engined Lancaster bomber III JA 913. The aircraft belonged to the no 8 (Pathfinder Force) Group Squadron no 83, and was involved in the early Battle of Berlin, taking part in a total of 22 sorties between 3 September and the end of November, but failed to return from a fourth consecutive raid on the night of 26/27 November 1943.

When V(ictory in) E(urope) Day came, virtually every house in Bacup sported a Union Jack from its window, with celebration parties, encouraged by the Board of Trade, who allowed the purchase of 'cotton bunting without coupons, as long as it is red, white or blue', and did not cost more than 1s 3d a square yard.

January 1945 was a cold month, and Bacup Co-operative Store delivery drivers turned out on a Sunday to distribute a total of 70 tons of coal in order to relieve the acute distress of some of their customers. Five days later 24 degrees (Fahrenheit) of frost were recorded.

Bread, though not rationed during the War, was rationed from 1946. It was in fact the first item to be de-rationed — in 1948, followed by clothes (1949), soap (10 September 1950), sweets (5 February 1953) and meat (1953). Rationing was finally ended completely in 1956. After the War, the Government was faced with a huge rehabilitation programme. Fifty temporary prefabricated houses at Blackthorn and Arcon estates were built, intended as a temporary measure, but actually lasting double their official life-span.

Meanwhile, 140 names on the memorial currently in the A.B. & D. Centre appear 'In honoured memory of Bacup members of the Armed Forces who gave their lives in the World War 1939-45'.

Ernest Sutton, a Salford city alderman, was responsible, along with James Ireland (of Maden & Ireland) and George Hardman (of Hardman Brothers of Waterfoot, and brother of William Hardman, historian) for instigating the City & Guilds course in footwear. In 1944 Sutton's was taken over by John Willie Johnson who took advantage of Sutton's machinery to expand his business, despite the rigid controls on wages, workforce levels and excess profits by the government. By 1949 the Johnson group was manufacturing over one million pairs of footwear a year with a turnover of £500,000.

The footwear industry received a further boost from the decision of Marks & Spencer to requisition slippers from Valley footwear firms, including Bacup Shoe Company Ltd and Maden & Ireland. And by 1950 the number of Bacup people employed in the slipper trade had peaked at 6,298.

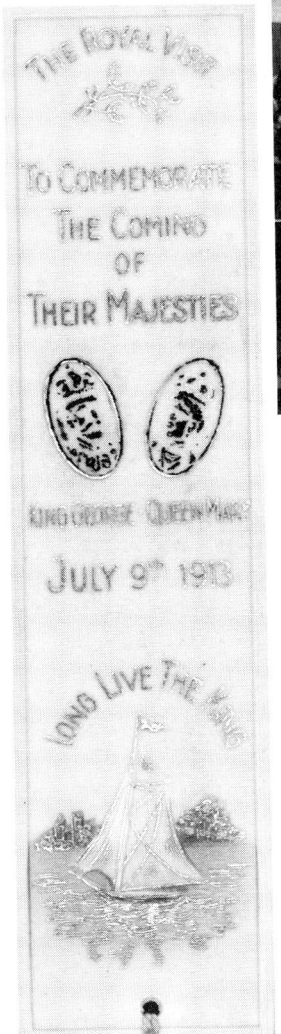

LEFT: Bookmark to commemorate the Royal visit. ABOVE: Royal visit to Bacup, 9 July 1913; the platform at Sandfield. BELOW: Postwar celebrations 1919, looking along St James Street from Bacup centre. The *J.H. Lord* fire engine B5930 can be seen, with the shops backing on to the river (cleared during the 1920s). Note the Union Jack flown from Sutcliffe's chemist's shop.

BOROUGH OF BACUP CENTRAL AID FUND.

GRAND CONCERT
Sunday, January 31st, at 8 p.m.
In the REGAL SUPER CINEMA,
Burnley Road, Bacup.
(By kind permission of the Valley Entertainments Ltd.)

FIRST-CLASS PROGRAMME.

Admission: One Shilling.
Proceeds in aid of above Fund.

TOP: Ticket for concert in 1926 in aid of the Central Aid Fund. ABOVE: HMS *Amaranthus* (K17), the ship adopted by Bacup as a result of Warships Week, February 1942. (IWM, negative no FL 1294) BELOW: Temporary houses being built on Arcon estate, October 1945; meant to last ten years, they stayed over 20. (BL)

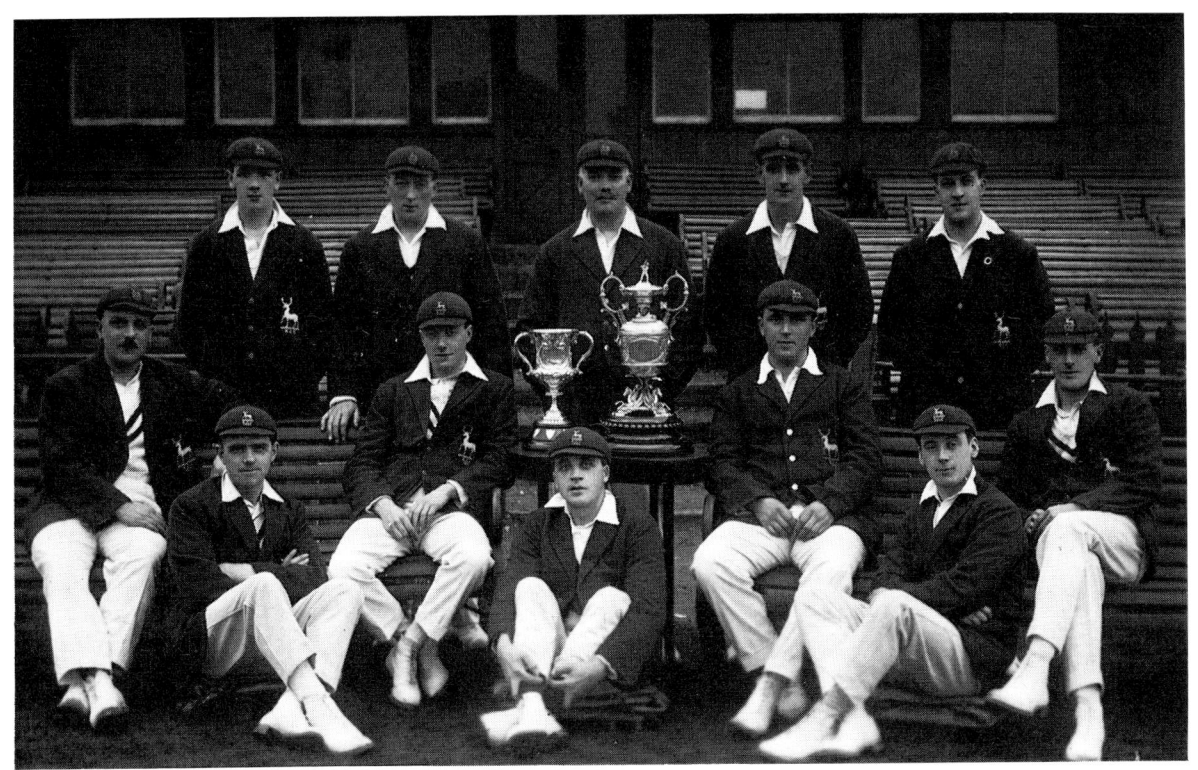

ABOVE: Bacup Cricket Club, Lancashire League champions and Worsley Cup winners, 1923. BELOW: Bacup Football Club, winners of the Lancashire Junior Cup 1910-11, beat Eccles 1-0 in the final at Rochdale.

Fun and Games

Leisure pursuits were scarce. Apart from Sundays, Good Friday and Christmas Day, there were few opportunities for leisure activities, although field days and annual tea parties organised by 19th-century Sunday Schools, plus Coronation or Jubilee celebrations, provided some entertainment. Leisure pursuits for working men included bull-baiting (outlawed 1835) at Hammerton Green, cock-fighting, pigeon flying, dog-racing and boxing. Bowls were also played, and still are today.

Judith Holt of Stubbylee records the coronation day of Queen Victoria on 28 June 1838 in her diary: 'Universal holiday. A procession of 6000 persons — Lodges, Sunday Scholars, Magistrates, Work people and their employers — Music, Flags, etc., a display hitherto unequalled in Bacup'.

Another diarist, Moses Heap, remarked after the Ten Hours Act of 1844 that previously 'it had been all bed and work; now in place of 70 hours a week we had 55½ hours. It became a practice, mostly on Saturday, to play games, especially football and cricket, which had never been done before'.

And in October 1844, the directors of Bacup's Mechanics' Institute urged shopkeepers 'to close at 9 o'clock in the evening', so that their assistants could have some free time for recreation.

The first sport to be organised was cricket, and in June 1860, Bacup Cricket Club was established, on land leased from landowner Rev James Heyworth. Cricket was regarded as a healthy pastime, by contrast with 'the heat and toil of our manufactories'. The first competition of the Lancashire Amateur Cricket Association in 1885 was won by Bacup, the only Rossendale entrant, who beat Darwen by 69 runs in the final. Bacup Cricket Club began its continuous membership of the Lancashire League in 1892, winning both championship and cup on six occasions, their most recent success being an emphatic nine-wickets victory in the 1993 Worsley Cup final.

Several Bacup players have turned out for county teams, while Dick Howorth (1909-1980) played for Worcestershire from 1933 to 1951, and in five Tests for England, taking a wicket with his first ball in test cricket, and making his highest test score in the same match. Bacup's most proficient professional, Everton de Courcy Weekes, gave immense enjoyment to Lancashire League spectators in general and Bacup in particular, as well as being in business as a sports outfitter.

Football followed a little later, Bacup Borough FC evolving from a team at the Irwell Springs Printing Works. William Mitchell, a proponent of physical fitness, praised football for its role in developing 'patience, perseverance, determination . . . [and] energy'. He also approved gymnastics, partly due to the influence of the Volunteers who linked the poor physique of many local men to the paucity of the national defences against any potential invaders.

The first links at Bacup Golf Club were officially opened on 2 July 1910. The Club moved to its present position at Bankside in 1916, and for seven years used a cottage in Dandy Row as a clubhouse. Par is 68 for the nine hole course of 5,652 yards.

Bacup's principal leisure interests have revolved around music and amateur dramatics. The brass band movement was essentially working-class, and band contests, especially Belle Vue (began 1853) and Crystal Palace (began 1860), were spin-offs from the Great Exhibition of 1851, intended to broaden horizons and stimulate ambitions. In 1858 Broadclough Old Band came on the scene and, after the formation of the Lancashire Rifle Volunteers in July 1859, became known as the 4th LRV Band, but evolved into the Bacup Old Band during 1862. Familiarly known as The Invincibles, the Band won four Open Championships at Belle Vue (1864, 1865, 1869, 1870), and by 1865 was acknowledged as the premier band in the country, but ceased after the death of tutor George Ellis in October 1871.

St John's Church Band began at Underbank School, merged into the Wellington Band, and subsequently became the Change Band in 1890, which in May won the first prize at Heap Bridge. In 1904 four local bands provided the music on Maden recreation ground during the summer — Irwell Springs, Change, Stacksteads, and Maden recreation ground's own boys' brass band. Bacup Schools formed a Band in 1923.

John Lumb's quartet of Bacup Handbell Ringers began when Irwell Terrace Band of Hope, established 1863 to help protect youngsters against the evils of drunkenness, bought a set of 53 handbells in May 1870 to attract interest to their meetings. After John Lumb died in 1896, his three colleagues, Abraham Pilling, James Henry Hoyle (tenor singer) and John W. Lord (bass), left Bacup.

Other musical bodies have included the Bacup Mechanics' Harmonic Society (1853); Stacksteads Wesleyan Prize Choir, which won an award at Crystal Palace in 1897; Bacup Temperance Choir (all millhands); Bacup Orchestral Society (1882-1970); Bacup Clef Club (1922-1934); the Wig and Gown string quartette and Bacup Male Voice Choir, formed 1932, which merged with the Bacup Choral Society and Bacup Ladies Choir in March 1936 to form the Bacup Choral Union, which broadcast at least twice on the North Regional Service. The Bacup and District United Baptist choir sang regularly during the inter-war years, and the Bacup and District Methodist United choir sang *The Messiah* every December until it ceased after the 1973 rendering.

Theatres appear to have begun with the Pickles Theatre in Newchurch Road in 1864, which accommodated 300 working men. This was followed in 1893 by the Royal Court Theatre up Rochdale Road, which had a capacity of 2,300, and was visited by David Lloyd George on Guy Fawkes Day 1904. The following year, a Bacup Amateur Dramatic Society was formed, making their debut in October 1907. Silent films appeared at the end of February 1913, under the heading of 'The Art Pictures', which became the Empire Theatre for the Christmas pantomime of 1918. Talking pictures arrived at the end of March 1930. In November 1936 the Empire Theatre was used for the first time by Waterside Amateur Operatic and Dramatic Society, founded in 1935, in 1937 becoming the Bacup AODS, whose highlight was the British premiere of *Camelot* in September 1967.

When the Church Street mill of Thomas Aitken ceased to function, it was replaced in March 1878 by the Bacup Public Hall and skating rink, also serving as the Rossendale Theatre, before becoming the Salvation Army barracks. A new Bacup skating rink was opened in June 1909, while shortly afterwards the Public Hall became the Gem Picture Palace, opened 1910, and later the Kozy Cinema. This was eventually demolished and replaced by the New Regal Cinema which opened 7 September 1931. This lasted for some 40 years, and subsequently became the New Embassy Bingo and Social Club.

The dramatic literature class of the Rossendale branch of the Workers' Educational Association spawned the Rossendale Players in 1936. St Mary's Amateur Dramatic Society started in 1953 and, as St Mary's Players, continue to stage plays, mainly comedies, each spring and autumn. Three three-act Lancashire comedy *A Bit o' Peace and Quiet*, by Bacup borough librarian John Vickers, was originally performed on 6 March 1954, and subsequently on ITV.

Just three teams of coconut dancers existed in Bacup before the Great War. Easter holidays in Rossendale generally resulted in all mills being closed from Thursday night until Tuesday morning, making Easter the obvious time for coconut dancing. Two teams, at Tunstead Mill and Lee Mill, operated simultaneously in the early 1880s, but after the collapse of the latter in 1886, James Mawdsley, a novice with only one year's experience at the time, joined the Tunstead Mill troupe, and later helped to start the Britannia Coconutters after the Great War.

Every Easter Saturday (and on other special occasions), the 'Nutters' dress up in white and red skirts, black breeches, white stockings, highly-polished black clogs with narrow toes, white caps with plumes, blackened faces, and wooden bobbin tops strapped to their hands and knees. They dance across town, banging the bobbins (their 'nuts') together, and are led by a 'whipper-in' to drive away evil spirits from the dancers' path and from the town. Their repertoire includes the Garland Dance (of which there are five separate varieties), and the Nut Dance (two dances), to the sound of the *Tip Toe Polka* (band accompaniment) or the *Shooting Star* (concertina accompaniment). Their garlands are hoops of cane decorated with red, white and blue crêpe paper, and the 'nuts' are made of maple wood.

The opening of Bacup Baths in 1893 coincided with the contemporary view that baths were as important in providing washing facilities as for recreation. The water was often so black it was impossible to see either the side or the bottom and anyone diving in disappeared completely. Attempts to purify the water only improved its colour to that of pale ale.

Two outstanding Bacup-born swimmers were David Billington (1885-1955) and Willie Foster (1890-1963), while 17-stone Walter Samuel Rockett, who on 22 August 1950 swam the English Channel from Dungeness (Cap Gris Nez) to Folkestone (Shakespeare Beach) in 14 hours 17 minutes, was a member of the Bacup swimming club water polo team in 1946.

Holidays were a development of the late Victorian era, aided by the establishment of a basic working week and Saturday half-days, along with the legislation of 1871 which led to August bank holidays. Half-day closing in Bacup on Tuesdays was mooted in 1873; and eight years later it was proposed that shops should close at 8 pm on three nights a week, with Tuesday afternoons off.

However, it took until just before the Great War for Bacup employers to agree with the textile and footwear unions on the details of local holidays. At one time the employers used to close whenever they chose, though in 1876 the Cotton Spinners Association agreed to close mills for a week during Whitsuntide.

In 1905 Bacup holidays comprised Easter Monday, the Friday and Saturday in Whit week, the Saturday following August Bank Holiday and the subsequent week, and Christmas Day. The following year employers were persuaded to adopt the fourth week in July as a standard annual holiday week — and even then without pay, though some workers benefited from 'clubs' which provided for holidays. In 1912 the local holiday list included Good Friday, the annual holiday week in July, and Christmas Day, and in July 1914 two extra days were added — at Whitsun and Christmas.

In 1915 local holidays in the footwear industry were brought into line with textiles at 13½ days. The two trades were to share the same holiday calendar thereafter.

Whit week thus became sacred to the footwear industry. There were other holidays too — Shrove Tuesday, for instance, featuring as a holiday in the school calendar up to 1931, and the day of the annual works outing, often in the new charabancs which made their appearance just before the Great War.

Leisure time frequently included organised trips to Blackpool, where Dr William Hardman (1845-1915), born in Bury, practised. When Blackpool paved many of its streets with stone setts, it created the impression of a transplanted mill town in places, leading him to refer in 1885 to 'Bacup by the beach . . .' The clatter of vehicles over the sett-paving gave guest-house owners cause to complain of noise, and some guests to feel ill as a result of the jolting.

Many churches had their scout groups, which began in the wake of Robert Baden-Powell's famous camp at Brightsea Island in 1907, and locally included such stalwarts as 'Pa' Chase, district scoutmaster during the 1930s, and John Finch, a scouter for over 50 years, after whom Finch Lodge in New Line is named. And in 1967 the 2nd Rossendale Scout Band began.

Bacup Floral and Horticultural Society had its first annual exhibition in the Mechanics' Institute on 24 November 1888, but soon disappeared. In May 1933, under the auspices of the Bacup Unemployed Workers' Allotment Society, the Allotment Holders Association was formed, had its first annual show in September 1933, its first annual chrystanthemum show in November 1937, and in 1962 was renamed the Bacup and District Horticultural Society.

Bacup Botanical Society, active by 1855, fostered a pre-occupation with instructive entertainment, while Bacup Natural History Society began in February 1878 and still continues, with lectures every winter Saturday evening, commencing with 'old Stacksteads' at the end of October, and concluding with 'Old Bacup' at the end of March.

The reduction and eventual abolition of newspaper duty, along with improved literacy, led to the production of reading matter and the provision of libraries. Bacup's first newspaper was the monthly *Bacup Chronicle & Rossendale Advertiser,* followed by the weekly *Bacup & Rossendale News* in May 1863, which began life as a liberal paper, but within two years was re-issued as a distinctively Conservative organ. The *Bacup Times* began in April 1865 as a Liberal alternative. *The Busy Body and Rossendale Critic* appeared in April 1876, amended its title to the *Rossendale Watchman* after five issues, but ceased publication five months later.

The best-known libraries were at Bacup Mechanics' Institute (5,209 volumes by 1898) and Bacup Co-operative Store, whose library opened in 1863 and had 11,226 volumes by 1899. In addition, the nine member schools of the Bacup Wesleyan Sunday School Union had a total of 4,545 volumes in 1893, and Ebenezer Baptists had a library of 300.

Workingmen's clubs, of which Bacup had ten at one time, also provided reading matter for their members, and Lord John Priestley (1849-1932), son of Enoch, and editor of the *Bacup Times* for 30 years, established a circulating library in the 1890s.

The Co-op library functioned until 1931 when its stock formed the nucleus of the Borough Public Library, opened on 27 June with an initial stock of 9,644 volumes. A record 1,740 books were issued at Bacup Library on 24 January 1942, and 274 volumes were issued in 75 minutes in the Junior library on 2 June 1942.

Dancing was catered for by the Ambulance Hall up Lanehead Lane (1925-1985), the Co-operative Hall (which in 1949 became the Embassy), and the Mechanics' Hall, whose upper floor was the venue for civic dances until the Bacup Leisure Hall was opened in December 1974.

Bacup Judo Club, formed in 1958, have since September 1980 occupied the upper floor of the Mechanics' Hall, while Bacup Library continues below.

ABOVE: Bacup Old Band, holders of 48 first prizes, 13 of them in succession, 1869-71. BELOW: Stacksteads Wesleyan Prize Choir, June 1897.

The cast photographed during rehearsal....

.... and some of the cast from 'Quaker Girl' – 1935

ABOVE: Empire Theatre 1993, with Forest House behind, and between them 'Plantation Promenade' — originally Plantation Street (Plant Back).
BELOW: Programme celebrating the 50th anniversary of Bacup 'Amateurs'.

LEFT: Britannia Coconut Dancers of Bacup: Nut Dance, Easter 1992. (SAH) RIGHT: Thomas Hampson, Bacup's own 'Pearly King', dressed in the suit stitched by himself and proudly worn on Carnival Day 1991. (TH) BELOW: Bacup Ambulance Hall — centre of St John Ambulance Brigade activity and a popular dancing centre for over half a century until wrecked by a gas explosion in 1985; a cluster of dwellings named St John's Court now occupies the site.

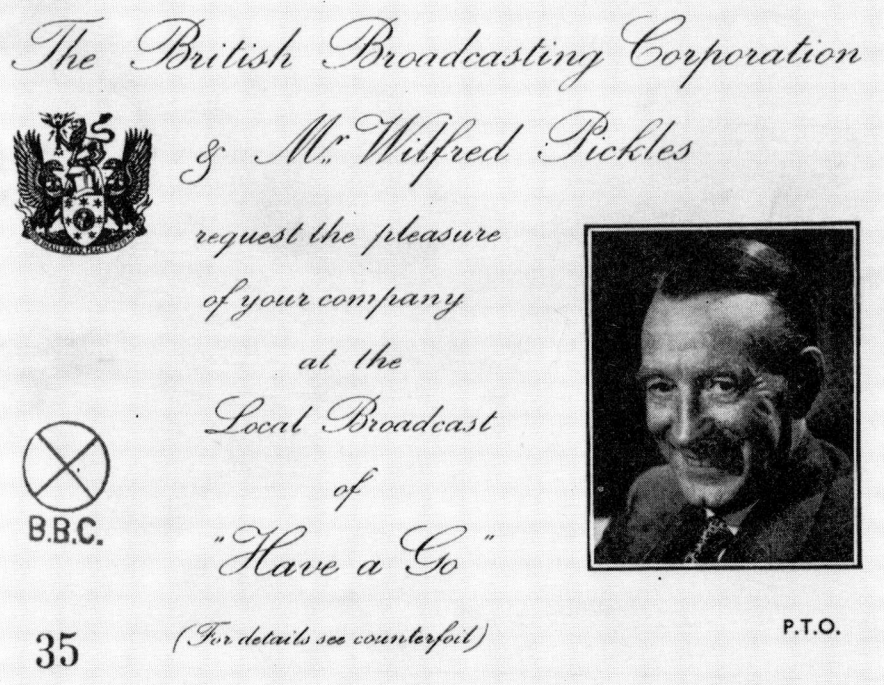

ABOVE: The 39th Aged, Blind & Disabled Treat — tea-time on Thursday, 23 May 1991 in Central Methodist school. (KRS) BELOW: Ticket for *Have-a-Go* — broadcast from the Mechanics' Hall, 3 December 1957.

The Last Forty Years

A traveller from a Manchester station was advised to take his 'seat in the dingiest of the dingy trains . . . retain [it] until you reach a terminus, and should it be raining, or should the smoke and stench in the atmosphere prove unbearable to the senses, be assured you have reached . . . Bacup'.

This poor visual image of Bacup was not helped in the early 1960s, when anyone travelling to Bacup by train and walking up to the town centre would have been disillusioned before arrival. The Market Street/Plantation Street area had become anything but attractive, and in 1964 Bacup's medical officer of health recommended demolition. This was done shortly afterwards in two stages.

But Bacup could never be accused of not looking after its elderly people. The Friday Club was officially formed in January 1942, when an informal arrangement allowed thirty pensioners (mainly men) to share food and fellowship together under the auspices of Ebenezer Baptist Church men's class. Two years later, property at the corner of Burnley Road and Goose Hill Street was bought and rented out at £1 a week. Membership was originally free, but in order to satisfy Inland Revenue, a charge of one penny a week (the price of a cup of tea) was introduced.

After the opening at the end of 1966 of the A.B. & D. Centre in the former Liberal Club, the Burnley Road equipment was transferred across the road, where members continue to meet on Friday afternoons, thus maintaining their identity and their name.

The first A.B. & D. Treat was held on Thursday, 4 June 1953, as part of the local celebrations for the Coronation. Entertainments were scheduled for four different places, with tea served in five venues. It was so successful that it became an annual event. Organisations and individuals were asked to guarantee subscriptions to a total minimum of £500 a year. It developed into each of the workpeople in Bacup's mills contributing one penny per week from their pay towards the Treat. In the first full year about 4,080 people contributed one penny each — a weekly average of £17, rising to £18 per week in 1959-60. Workers in Bacup's industries still contribute a minimum of one penny per week from their pay, though donations from Bacup Rotary Club now help to fund the Treat.

In May 1955 Bacup had the opportunity of twinning with the French town of Mussidan in the Dordogne, but considered it too distant. Bellac (250 miles south of Paris) was thought too remote, Bacup preferring a town nearer the Channel coast. Not long afterwards, Bacup were twinned with Bocholt, from where a party of eleven youngsters visited Bacup in the spring of 1952 — a mere seven years after the end of hostilities. Some of them were uncertain what kind of a reception they would find, but they met nothing but friendship and understanding — a quality which more than compensates for the weather.

On average it rains in Bacup on 230 days a year, but flooding is not now as major a problem, though one great downpour on 8 August 1967 wrecked the last lodging house in

Bacup — Raby's on King Street. Bacup's average rainfall for 1965-67 rose to 69.44 inches — while the winter of 1962-63 was the coldest this century and the year of the big freeze.

The first Soroptimist Club was formed at Oakland in California in July 1921. Soroptimism, roughly defined as 'the best of sisters', is akin to Rotary. The Bacup club came into being in 1961. Other ladies' interests are catered for by Bacup Inner Wheel, the Ladies Guild (Townswomen's Guild from 1963 to 1980), and the Inskip League of Friendship, which looks after the social interests of the disabled.

The Citizens' Advice Bureau was revived in September 1966 to serve Bacup and Whitworth, and the following year Bacup's first Oxfam shop came into being, at which time ten welfare organisations were recorded, 17 religious ones, and 31 sports organisations. The Bacup Civic Society, formed in the spring of 1971, stemmed from a concern over the destruction of many local beauty spots.

The demolition of Thorn House in April 1946 heralded a new council estate on Fairview. However, it was plagued by undesirable elements and acquired a notorious reputation which spread far beyond Bacup. An estates working party was set up to deal with the problem. During 1983 the name was changed to Pennine Road, and a few other streets were re-named. Between October 1980 and the summer of 1991, the area benefited from the presence of the Sisters of the Good Shepherd, whose five nuns staffed a Family Centre known as Sunnycrest. Their pioneering work helped to moderate the previous bad image, and is also enhanced by the young morris dancers of the Bacup Starlite Troupe, formed 1991.

Spurgeon's Child Care have continued and expanded the work of the Sisters, aided by a Detached Families' Worker funded largely by the Church Urban Fund and the Bacup Against Crime action group — which is supported by the Bacup and Stacksteads Estate Management Board, comprising eight tenants, five from Bacup plus three from Stacksteads, two owner-occupiers and five councillors. The main concerns of local residents are unemployment — the Pennine Road estate having the highest unemployment rate of any area within the local parliamentary constituency — crime (especially burglary), vandalism, litter and graffiti. The lack of entertainment for young people has been a perennial cry since the Empire Theatre and the Regal Cinema closed for their original purposes.

Judicious demolitions and sensitive landscaping, along with a 15-year council plan to create smokeless zones on housing estates between 1972 and 1987, stemming from the Clean Air Act of 1957, have helped to restore some of Bacup's character. Since 1962 over two thousand dwellings have been demolished in slum clearances, while new private housing estates have been developed throughout Bacup, along with the erection of Springfield Court under the aegis of the Anchor Sheltered Housing Association.

In August 1935 a new semi-detached stone-fronted house on Greensnook Lane cost £450. The price of a £7,000 house in 1966 escalated to £70,000 by 1986 — a rise of 1,000% in twenty years. Rossendale's average house prices are the highest in East Lancashire, a by-product of the opening of the M66, but still considerably less than the average house price in the North-West.

In 1976 local builder John Nixon erected twenty three-bedroomed town houses at Greenend, billing them as the cheapest in the country at £6,995 each. Two years earlier, the same builder described his own house as the most expensive ever to be offered for sale in Bacup. Erected in 1972, the four/five-bedroomed detached house in Oaken Close was on the market at £29,500.

In January 1964 the last cotton mill in Bacup ceased to function. Factory closures, enforced redundancies and subsequent unemployment during the late 1970s and early 1980s were devastating in their effect on family life. In 1976, 475 people (348 men and 127 women) were in Bacup's dole queue, and by the end of the 1970s the total unemployed was registered at 455 — over half the total Rossendale figure of 948; but during 1980 the figure reached 1 in 4, Bacup having twice as many unemployed as the rest of the Valley where the overall unemployment rate was 7.6%. In 1981 the figure was double, prompting the formation of an Unemployed Workers' Centre as a meeting-place for those out of work. During 1989 and 1990 the three Bacup wards saw the highest unemployment in Rossendale, while in April 1992, Bacup's jobless stood at 730. In January 1991, Bacup Credit Union was set up to help people caught in a debt trap.

Ironically, as the standard of post-war living began to improve, the number of department stores taking better-quality footwear increased.

In 1976 E. Sutton & Sons expanded into the only purpose-built footwear factory in Bacup — at Riverside, on the site of India Mill and the railway station. During 1977 Bacup was reported to have the highest concentration of shoe factories in England, providing jobs for half the available workforce, but unfair competition from the Far East, where wages amounted to mere handfuls of rice, was beginning to have a damaging effect, and in 1982 Olive Mill closed, followed by New Hey Mill in July 1988, and Stacksteads Mill in May 1990.

However, a truncated Bacup Shoe Company still supplies slippers to Marks & Spencer from their Atherton Holme Mill, and there remains a gut feeling that the footwear industry can survive in the face of cheap foreign competition, rising unemployment, and the lack of government help.

Stacksteads Mill has become the Tollbar Business Park, and other mills have also diversified into sectionalised industries. There are also nine industrial estates of varying sizes around Bacup.

After the Second World War, local churches entered a period of retrenchment, and today there are just 16 left in the whole of the Bacup and Stacksteads area — four Anglican, four Methodist, and four Baptist among them.

Mount Pleasant Wesleyans merged with Waterside as Central Methodist Church in December 1951. Irwell Terrace and Zion Baptists united as Union Baptist Church in June 1948, being joined in November 1962 by Ebenezer, the three-in-one amalgamation becoming Trinity Baptist Church, which used the Irwell Terrace chapel and the Zion schoolroom until dry rot caused the demolition of the former; the erstwhile Zion school premises were refurbished to serve as Bacup's principal Baptist church.

Little trace remains of Mount Pleasant and Ebenezer. The two sets of buildings with their respective graveyards, situated prominently on either side of Earnshaw Road, were demolished in 1952/3 and 1964/5 respectively and the area landscaped.

Bacup Co-operative Society went out of existence as a separate entity in 1959 when it amalgamated with Rochdale Pioneers' Equitable Society, who two years later opened the Krazy Kuts supermarket in Union Street.

The market was transferred to 'temporary' open premises in Temple Court on 30 May 1956, where it has remained ever since. Re-furbished and reconstructed in August 1972, Bacup market operates on Wednesdays and Saturdays, and since 1989 a flea market has been held on Fridays.

On St George's Day 1960, Bacup became the smallest local authority in the country to operate a mobile library service, and the three successive vehicles performing this function served for all but 31 years, having issued a grand total of 967,162 books during that time.

The 1970s saw the appearance of the *Bacup Echo* (1972-77), and the acquisition of a Royal Warrant by a Bacup firm. Windsor Castle ordered a supply of underlay from Bury Masco Industries, who had recently ceased its production. Gaskell's were near neighbours and made a similar product, which they began to supply to both Windsor Castle and Buckingham Palace. After three years' regular supply, they were entitled to a ten-year Royal Warrant,

ABOVE: Bacup Starlite junior morris dancers, winners at Reddish Carnival 1993. (RC)(2) BELOW: 2nd Rossendale Scout Band, formed 1967, here in front of Stubbylee Hall, April 1980. (RAB)

for which Gaskell's successfully re-applied in 1987, entitling them to display outside their premises at Lee Mill the crest 'By Royal Appointment'.

Bacup has a reputation for good work. One Scottish visitor pushed several pairs of scissors through a King Street letter-box at 2 am one Saturday morning, so that she could take them home next day. Though she could have had them sharpened in Glasgow, she preferred the superior service of Lord & Taylor.

Everton Weekes revisited Bacup in the summer of 1976 and admitted that Bacup had changed a lot — 'it is a much cleaner and nicer place now, with a lot of the grubbiness demolished'.

The image of Stacksteads has also improved. The Brandwood area was considered one of the worst examples of dereliction in Lancashire. A major project in the early 1980s reclaimed 119 acres of land despoiled by industrial activity and neglect, though in the process irreplaceable historical evidence was destroyed.

Rebuild or Restore

A photograph taken early in 1924 shows a single-decker Todmorden Corporation motor 'bus struggling to negotiate the corner from Yorkshire Street past the old George & Dragon Inn at the bottom of Lanehead.

During the next few years the whole of the Townhead property was demolished. Joshua Thomas Hoyle bought up the shops which stood on the brink of the River Irwell in St James Street, and helped to pay towards the cost of covering over the open part of the river. The Maden memorial was transferred to Stubbylee Park, and the area formerly bounded by Stewart Street, Bridge Street and Yorkshire Street to the foot of Lanehead Lane was renamed St James Square. At the same time Bacup Corporation acquired the Angel Inn, at the time the oldest hostelry in town, and which had closed its doors in 1924.

Some years earlier, in 1911, the Bulls Head Inn was demolished to facilitate road widening at the bottom of Burnley Road, which at the time was still known as Church Street. In its place was built the King George V hotel, opened in December 1912, which at the time of the Royal visit in 1913 was reputedly the only hostelry in the country to bear the name of the then reigning monarch. The Queen's Hotel was where it still stands at the corner of Yorkshire Street and Lanehead Lane, and between them was the Angel, leading to a local joke that 'only the Angel came between the King and the Queen'. From 1945 to 1947 the landlord of the King George V was William Waddington, father of Percy Sugden of Coronation Street. It closed as a licensed hostelry in October 1983.

All the properties between the two 'royal' hotels were acquired and demolished as part of the Townhead redevelopment scheme. On the site of the former Angel Inn one of F. W. Woolworths red-brick multiple stores opened to the public on 26 August 1932 and ceased to trade on 28 June 1986. Between Woolworths and the King George V Hotel was erected a splendiferous Electricity Showroom, designed by Waterfoot architect Albert Brocklehurst, and opened just before Christmas 1938. The former Bacup coat of arms still adorns the building. Its design was a prototype for a potential wholesale redevelopment of everything between Lee Street and St James Square.

In 1936, ostensibly to improve the junction of Market Street and Burnley Road, Bacup Corporation set out to acquire the block of property bounded by Temple Court, Market Street, and St James Square. A few years later a writer in Mount Pleasant *Greetings* felt that the salvation of Bacup lay in a bold policy of complete reconstruction and development.

He would have widened St James Street from Irwell Terrace chapel to the District Bank, laying out the area thus cleared as municipal gardens with bandstand, remodelling the interior of the Mechanics Hall to make an Opera House, and converting the market hall into an aquarium and skittle alley.

Some of these proposals seem remarkably like Albert Brocklehurst's comprehensive plans for Bacup centre in 1939 — grand avenues of shops and offices, plus municipal buildings, concert hall, and bus station.

But just over five weeks later, Adolf Hitler marched into Poland. The outbreak of war meant that nothing could be spent on town centre redevelopment unless it was considered essential to the war effort, and the whole scheme was shelved. But in 1952 the town centre roundabout replaced the open cobbled square which had been there since the demolition of the Townhead property in the late 1920s. It was enhanced by the fountain donated by Bacup Amateurs to mark the 1953 Coronation.

In 1958, the Borough Engineer resurrected the pre-war proposals for improving the junction of St James Street and Market Street, and in 1960 recommended the 'compulsory acquisition and demolition of all property betwen Barclays Bank and Union Street and fronting Market Street, St James Square and St James Street, with redevelopment as shops and offices by a privately owned development company'.

A new link road from Market Street to the bottom of Rochdale Road envisaged the demolition of all the property in the Lee Street and Industrial Place area. As late as 1974 this was seen as 'the lynchpin of plans to reshape the town centre road system' and at that time would have cost an estimated £119,500.

Consequently many Bacup shopkeepers felt threatened by planning blight and the potentially high rents likely under any town centre redevelopment scheme. An article in *Lancashire Life* considered Bacup town centre dreary and anonymous.

Eighteen months later, Prime Minister Harold Wilson urged local authorities to consider improving the environment and efficiency by measures *not* involving large scale rebuilding, but rather by 'the conservation of the distinctive atmosphere and character of town centres', a move heartily supported by Bacup Property Owners' Association, and the Civic Amenities Act of 1967.

In practice, nothing further transpired until local government reorganisation in 1974, when the priorities and pre-occupations of the new Rossendale Borough Council majored on land reclamation, industrial development and conservation. And it was the conservation potential of the centre of Bacup which gripped the imagination of Planning Officer Ian Goldthorpe, who saw Bacup as 'probably one of the best remaining examples of a small Lancashire cotton town'. His vision was rewarded by the designation of Bacup town centre in December 1981 as a Conservation Area, becoming the blue-print for an area plan four years later which sought to 'conserve, protect and enhance' the 'Victorian heritage'. A few months later a programme of environmental landscaping began in Irwell Terrace, the beginning of what is now an open paved area constructed of Yorkshire flags, lamp standards, street furniture and 'bus shelter in cast iron, reproduced in Victorian detail in an attempt to 'preserve the olde worlde charm' of Bacup town centre.

The sketch map of Bacup Conservation area formed the basis of a stroll around Bacup in 1983. It was extended in June 1990 at the behest of English Heritage, the better-known name of the Historic Buildings and Monuments Commission, which concerns itself with listed buildings. They made it a condition of their participation and funding that Bacup Conservation area should be extended to include properties in the Dale Street area, plus commercial properties in Todmorden Road and Rochdale Road. They funded the Bacup project for a three-year period (1990-1993).

Bacup Conservation area embraces 16 officially listed buildings, all Grade II, with the exception of Forest House, the sole Grade II* item, now turned into an old peoples' home and unhistorically renamed 'The Laurels'. Grade II* buildings possess especially unusual or interesting features such as interior detail and ornate plaster work, though some interior vandalism around 1975 destroyed the character of the staircase at Forest House. In all there are 80 listed buildings in Bacup.

One of them is the old Market Hall, adjacent to which is a building familiar to viewers of the BBC TV *Juliet Bravo* series as the Hartley police station. Diagonally across the old market ground and behind some railings is a small enclosed ground plainly designated ELGIN ST, reputedly the shortest street in the country. A plan dated 1854 shows a plot of building land of 292⅔ square yards at the corner of Bankside Lane and Lord Street, familiarly known as Crey Bottoms or Crey Holme. Elgin Street first appeared on a map in 1893, was occupied by residents for some 60 years, and has since July 1973 belonged to the owner of Brookes Studio (or Elgin Workshops). Since the publication of the 1987 *Guinness Book of Records,* it has been officially recorded as the shortest street in the world, let alone Bacup, at exactly 17 feet long.

Yorkshire Street was ripe for modernisation. Since the demolition of the old Corn Mill in July 1952, remaining properties had fallen into considerable disrepair. Where the corn mill stood is now Bacup Health Centre, opened 22 April 1974. After the retirement at the end of 1987 of Bacup's last clogger, English Heritage sponsored the refurbishment and renovation of the odd-numbered properties in Yorkshire Street, which were officially opened on 8 September 1989 by the then local MP David A. Trippier, in his capacity as Minister for the Environment and Countryside. Other properties in Bacup centre have benefited from similar treatment; and eleven more self-contained flats have been constructed above the electricity showrooms, in keeping with the 'Living over the shop' policy.

However, since the Yorkshire Street scheme was completed, all five shops have seen changes, and not all are still occupied. Business failures are due not so much to the conservation initiative, as to the economic recession and the fact that refurbished properties attract *new* enterprises which, unfortunately, seem prone to a disquietingly high failure rate.

The new Bacup Saver Store was erected under conservation conditions in Irwell Street and opened on 15 November 1988. Properties at the bottom of Rochdale Road (19-27) were converted into self-contained flats, and the former cellar dwellings in Industrial Place were converted into five self-contained shop units which proudly proclaim their custom, though some of these have also found the economic difficulties of the early 1990s impossible to absorb. The Industrial Place properties were originally the subject of Closing Orders imposed by the former Bacup Council in March 1935 — 56 years earlier.

In the autumn of 1992, Janet Anderson, the new MP, laid the foundatoin stone of a £2.7 million development for the Manchester & District Housing Association on Tong Lane — 56 flats, bungalows and houses, constructed by local builders in natural stone and slate to match the rest of the Bacup conservation area. This latter development embodies the outer wall which had remained, incongruously propped up, from the former Yorkshire Street (Tong) Mill owned for 62 years by Howard & Hargreaves and subsequently by Icon Impressions prior to its demolition earlier in the year.

Sandstone cobbled setts were the standard street surfacing material locally until the 1930s. It has been suggested that cobblestones help reduce vehicle speed, and in the Bacup Conservation area they may be seen at Bank Street (up to the police station), Bath Street (off Rochdale Road), and Rose Street (off Bankside Lane) in particular.

More town centre properties have undertaken conservation initiatives, each one bearing a plaque during the period of refurbishment intimating that the work was being carried out on behalf of English Heritage, and financially supported by them. Beatrice Potter in 1866 suggested that 'Hebden Bridge resembles Bacup in its fusion of the working and lower middle classes'. Could Bacup become the East Lancashire equivalent of Hebden Bridge in its attraction for tourists?

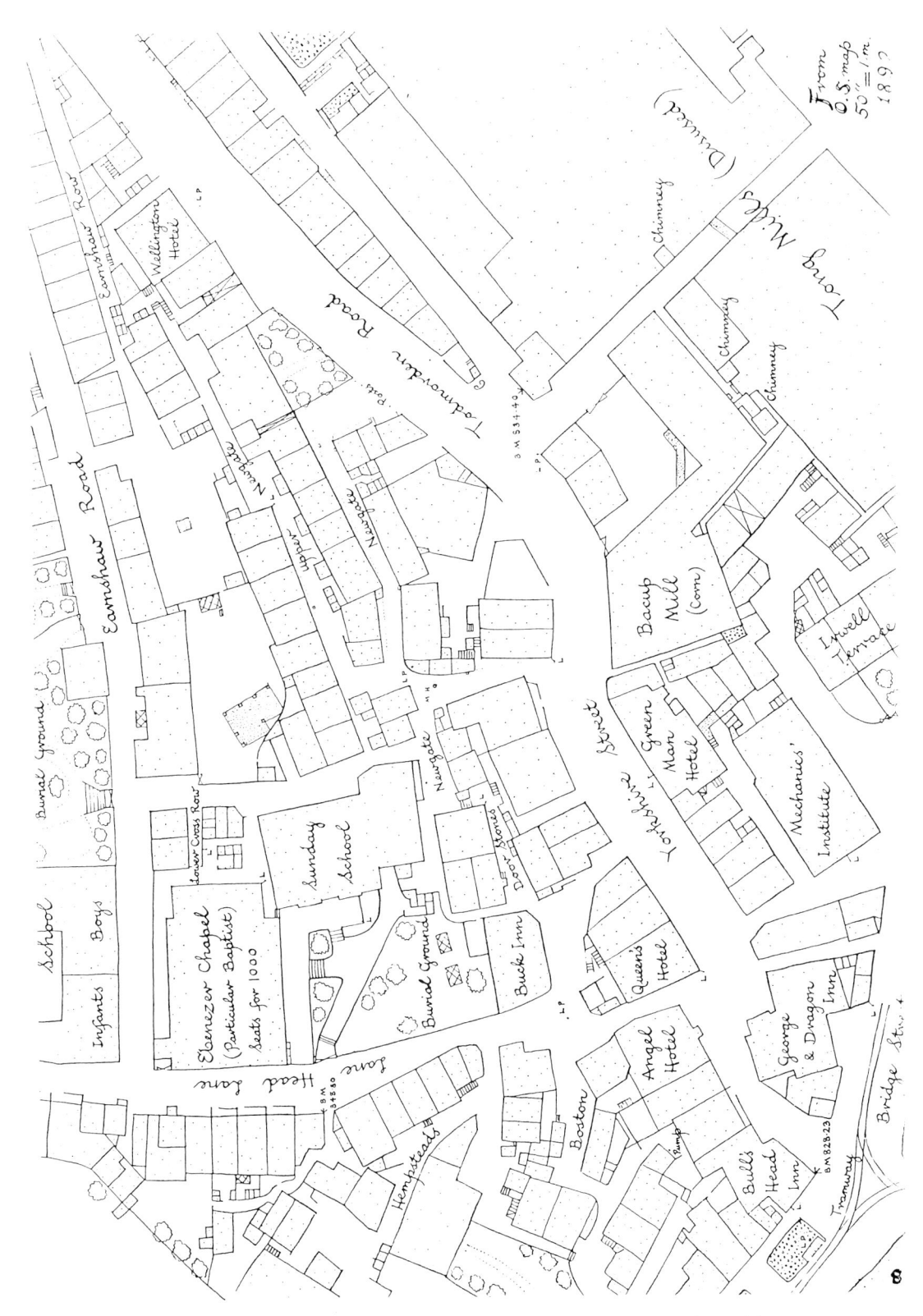

Part of the 1892 Ordnance Survey map, redrawn, bears comparison with
the map on the back end-paper. (JBT)

118

ABOVE: 1924: a single-deck Todmorden Corporation 'bus tries to negotiate the corner between the George & Dragon Inn and Lanehead — a task which led to the clearance of the Townhead property in Bacup centre. BELOW: A view of the Townhead property from Yorkshire Street c1924; the Queen's Hotel is on the right, with the King George V clock tower just visible beyond it, and Young J. Ashworth's greengrocery stall to the left.

ABOVE: Townhead property looking up Stewart Street to the Queen's Hotel c1924; St John's Church is in the distance, and the property shown comprises the even numbers on Bridge Street. BELOW: Proposed civic centre, with the old market hall and Market Street on the right, and all other property between there and St James Street completely redeveloped, 1939. (MJO)

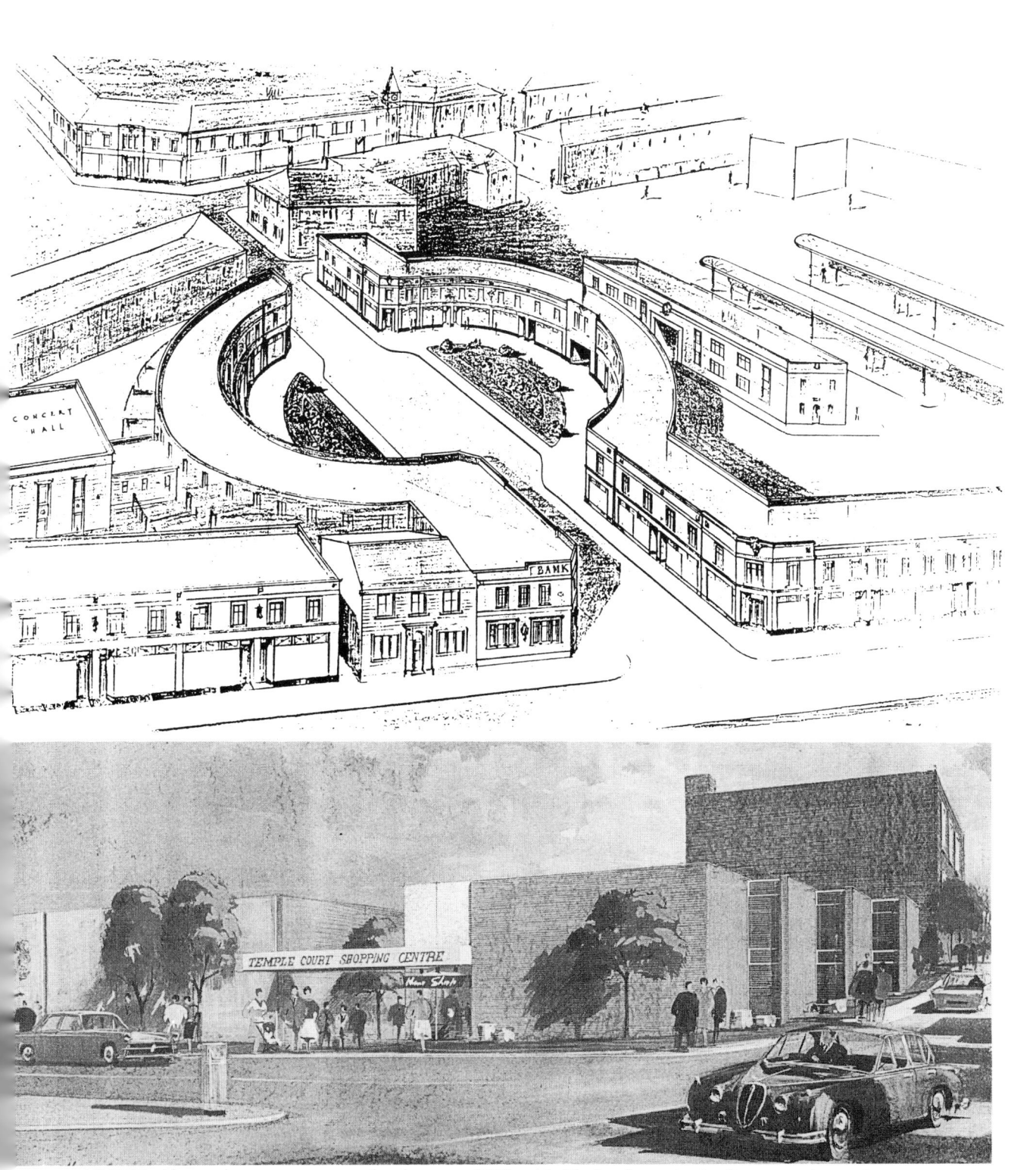

ABOVE: Alternative town centre redevelopment 1939, with Market Street in the foreground, new 'bus station and concert hall. (MJO) BELOW: As Bacup might have become if a scheme c1960 had been implemented — with a Temple Court shopping centre giving access to where the open market currently operates, and Barclays Bank on the right. (MJO)

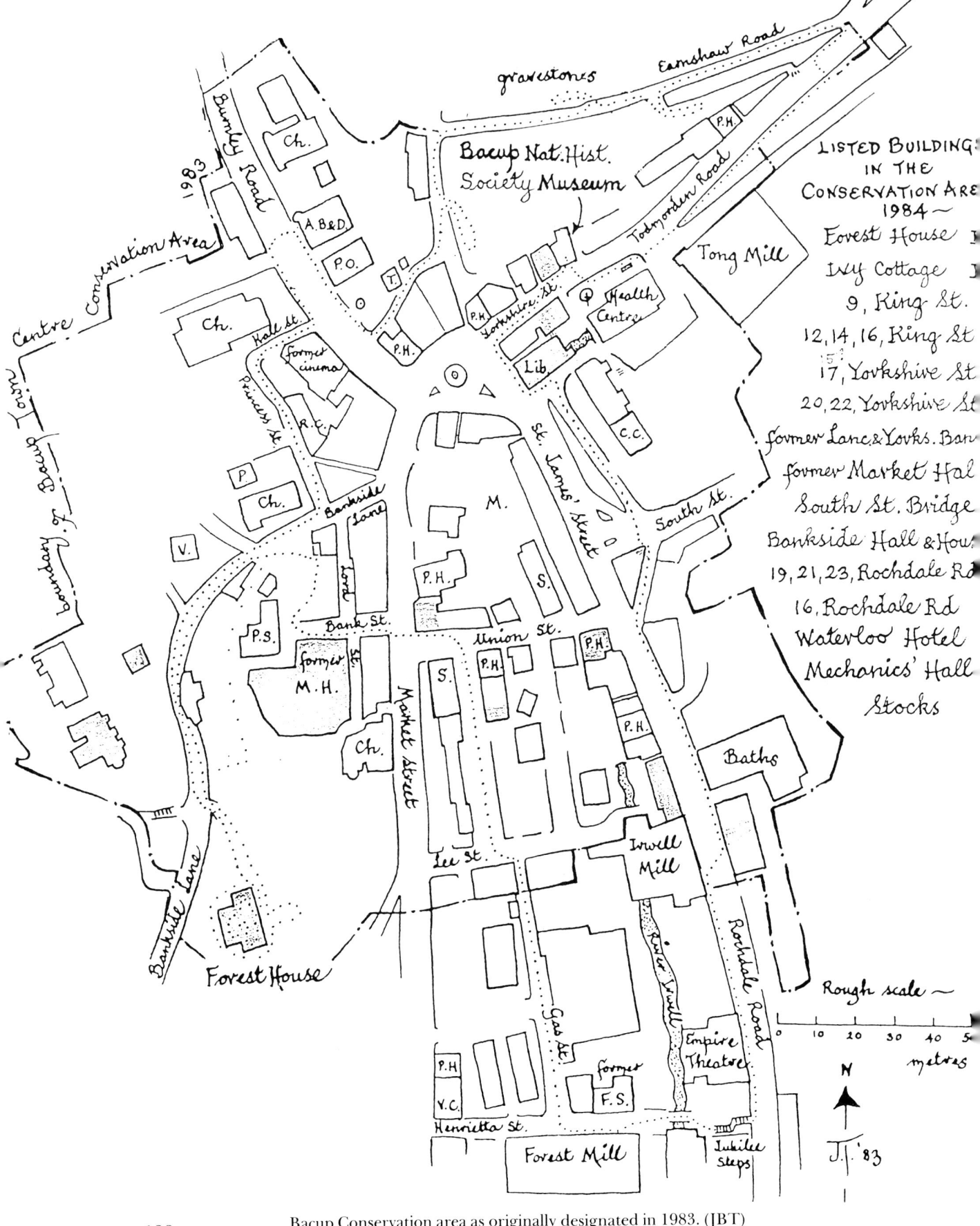

Bacup Conservation area as originally designated in 1983. (JBT)

LEFT: Model of Elgin Street, the shortest street in the world, crafted by Bryan Ellis for Brookes Studio 1992. (NBN) BELOW: Industrial Place, showing Bacup Heritage Office and the top floors of the former takin' in weavers' loom shops, 1993. RIGHT: Bill Meller, Bacup's last clogger, in characteristic pose — he believes clogs are/were warm(er), sturdier and more waterproof than ordinary boots and shoes. (WM)

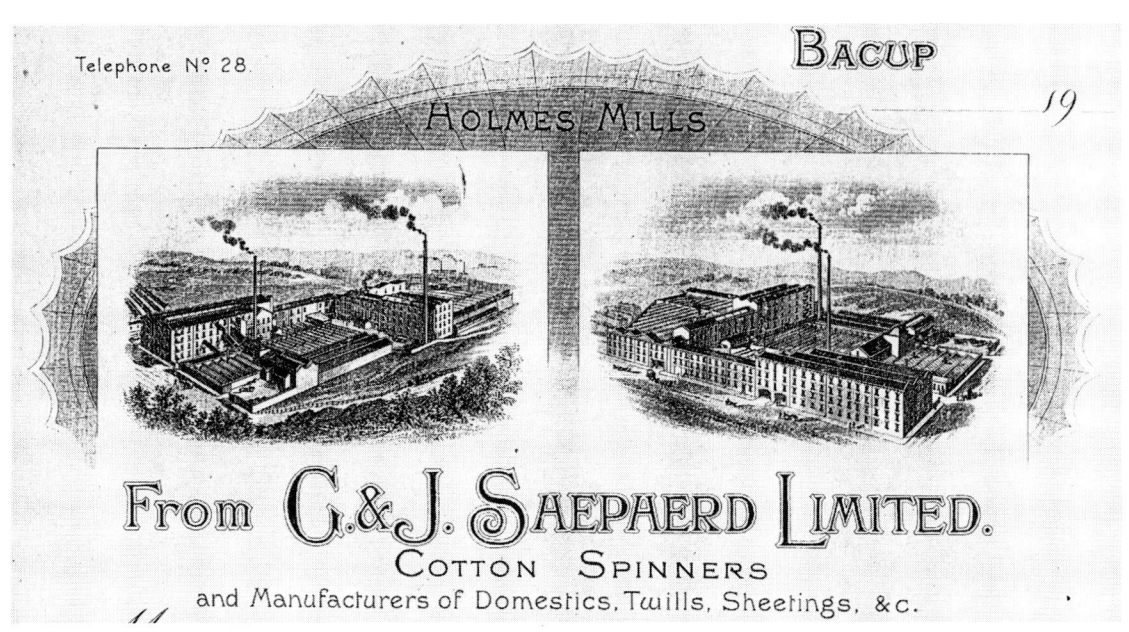

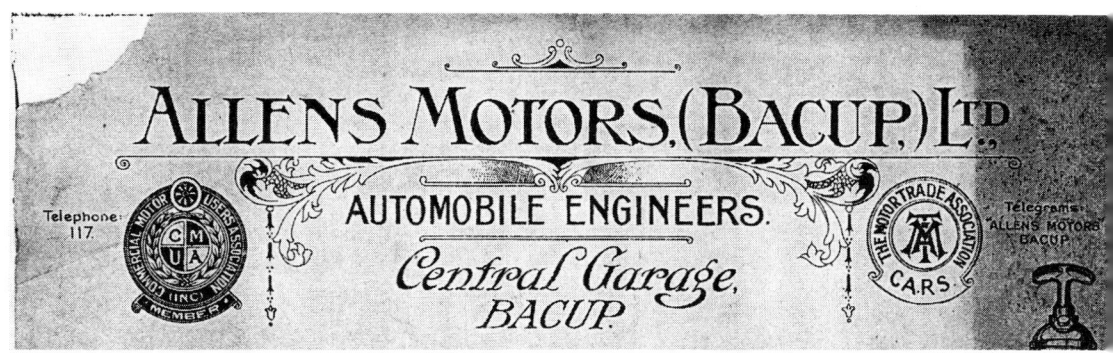

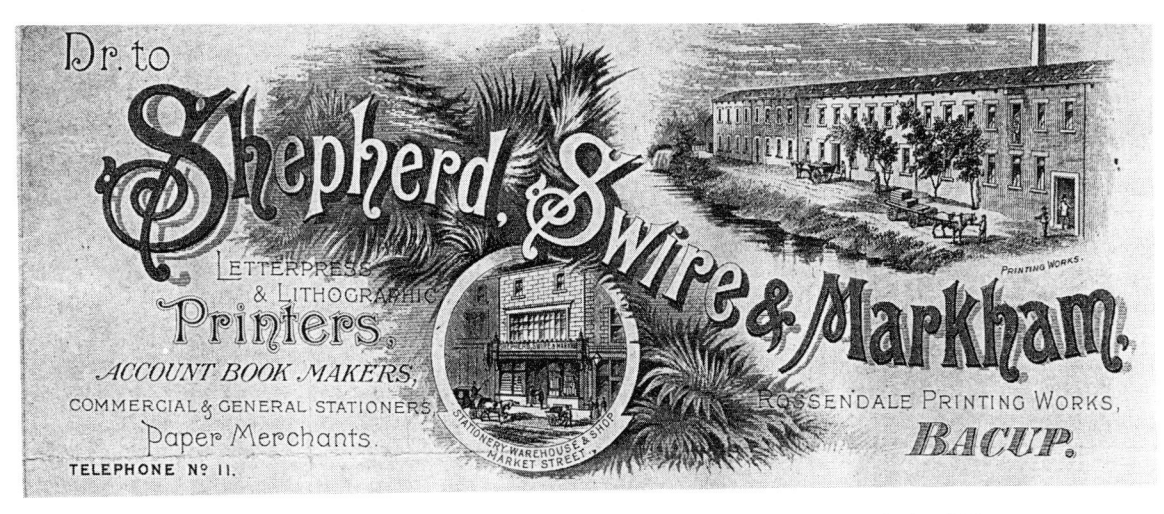

Letterheads from Bacup firms; only Allen's Motors remain in 1993.

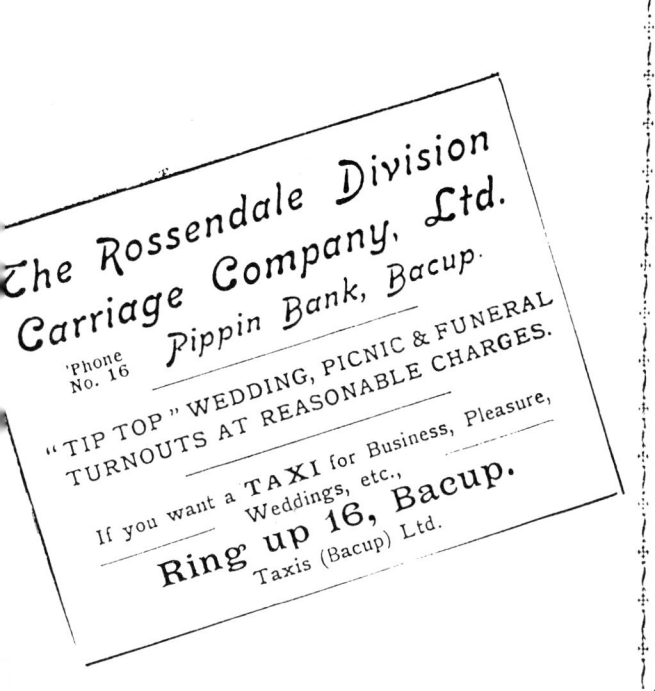

The Rossendale Division Carriage Company, Ltd.
Pippin Bank, Bacup.
'Phone No. 16

"TIP TOP" WEDDING, PICNIC & FUNERAL TURNOUTS AT REASONABLE CHARGES.

If you want a TAXI for Business, Pleasure, Weddings, etc.,

Ring up 16, Bacup.
Taxis (Bacup) Ltd.

**The Fish Shop
Union Street
Bacup**
Tele. 686

ALSO MOBILE SHOP

ARTHUR SHELTON

For Quality and Service

Fresh Fish daily direct from Coast

Fresh Frozen Foods
Wall's Sausages and Pies

☞ Customers can watch us make their Shoes if they like.

THE
STANDARD BOOT SHOPS

6, MARKET STREET, BACUP, & 24, BANK STREET, RAWTENSTALL.

Read the following Testimonial:

BROADCLOUGH, BACUP,
October 9th, 1891.

To th' Maister o' th' Standard Boot Shop.

"You con make me another pair like last, an' if they're done as weel aw shoon'd grumble. Yo'n done for me seven yers, an' they'n all turned water, an' kept mi feet dry; an' am i' all sooarts o' weather, an' on th' moors amang th' gress an' dew an' snow."

JORDAN RAWSTRON, Rossendale Hunt Keeper.

We make and repair Boots and Shoes with Waterproof Leather, and it wears like iron.

Gent's Boots from 4s. 11d. to 16s. 6d.
Ladies' ,, ,, 2s. 6d. to 14s. 6d.

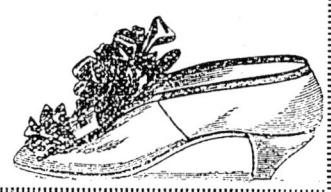

ABOVE & OVER: Adverts for seven Bacup businesses; Shelton's remains in the family 1993, but all the others have ceased.

Select Bibliography

Allen, Thomas. *Quarterly Reports*, 1877-1881
Bacup Co-operative Society Store Ltd.: Centenary 1847-1947
   Corporation: *Education Committee minutes;*
     Full Council minutes
     Official handbooks
   Corporation Fire Brigade: *Reports of fires within the borough of Bacup, 1894-1907*
   St. John's Church: *Bacup parish church historical survey and handbook*, 1935
   St Mary's Catholic Church: *The Catholics in Bacup, 1852-1952*
   Savings Committee: *Wings for Victory National Savings Campaign*, 1943: Aircraft log book of Lancaster JA. 913
   School Board: *Minutes*
   Wesleyan Methodist Circuit: *Quarterly Meeting minute book, 1858-1883*
Beulah Methodist Church, Britannia: *Centenary souvenir, 1852-1952*
Bolton, Charles A. *Salford diocese and its Catholic past: a survey.* 1950
Bowden, K. F. *Samuel Chadwick and Stacksteads.* 1982
Brandwood Survey, 1820.
Buckland, Theresa Jill. *Ceremonial dance traditions in the South-West Pennines and Rossendale*, (Leeds Univesity thesis 1984)
Cecil, Robert. *Four Lancashire families*, typescript, undated
Census returns, 1841, 1851, 1861, 1871, 1881, 1891.
Chadwick, Edwin. *Report on the sanitary conditions of the labouring population*, 1842
Chapman, Eve. *The Darney societies*, edited by Ralph Wilkinson, 1970
Craven, Harry and Digby, Ronald Y. compilers: *A Bacup Miscellany*, 1972
Davies, John. *Bacup's hotels, inns, taverns and beerhouses*, 199-
Deegan, Judith. *The Yellow road: a history of Yelloway Motor Services Ltd*, 1982
Duckworth, Sir James. *Autobiography*, unpublished manuscript, 1910
Farrer, William. *The Court rolls of the Honor of Clitheroe*; 3 vols. 1897-1913
Fishwick, Henry. *The History of the parish of Rochdale in the county of Lancaster*, 1889
Geddes, Sandie. *John Brett: from Clopton to Bacup*, 1991
Griffith, L.D. *Tunstead, 1840-1940: a short history*, 1940
Hardman, Willie. *History of Waterfoot*, 1922?
Hargreaves, Harold. *various scrapbooks relating to transport*
   James. *The Life and memoir of the late Rev. John Hirst* . . . 1816
Hartley, Eric. *The Development of education in Rossendale,. 1870-1914* (M.Ed. thesis 1962)
History of the Bacup Old Band and a list of prizes won . . . 1908
Hitchen, Veda. *Almost a century (1895-1986), a history of Thorn County Primary School, Bacup*, 1986
Holgate & Roberts (Solicitors). *To the ratepayers of Bacup and the neighbourhood*, 1854
Howarth, Peter. *Aspects of educational, cultural, and leisure provision in Bacup . . . 1860-1910: a thesis submitted . . . for the degree of Master of Education* . . . 1979
Humberston, Alfred. *St Saviour's Church, Bacup: a brief historical guide* 1992
Irwell Springs (Bacup); Band. *Established 1864: a record of fifty years.* 1914
Jessop, William. *An Account of Methodism in Rossendale and the neighbourhood* . . . 1880
Johnson, L. N. *A Brief history of Bacup fire brigade.* 1983
Lee, William. *Report to the General Board of Health on a preliminary enquiry into the sewerage, drainage, and supply of water, and the sanitary condition of the inhabitants of Bacup*, 1849
   Report to the General Board of Health on a preliminary enquiry into the sewerage, drainage, and supply of water, and the sanitary condition of the inhabitants of the Chapelry District of Bacup, in the county of Lancaster, 1850
Macdonald's Directory of Rochdale, Milnrow, Littleborough, Rossendale . . . 1879
Mannex & Co. publishers. *History, topography, and directory of mid-Lancashire* . . . 1854
   Directory and topography of North East Lancashire, vol. II 1876
Mather, J. Marshall. *Rambles round Rossendale (1st and 2nd series, 1888 and 1894)*
Maxim, James L. *Pack-horse and other ancient tracks in and around Rochdale* . . . 1927

Mechanics' Hall, Bacup. *directors' minute books and annual reports, 1839-1909*
Mount Pleasant Wesleyan Sunday School centenary souvenir, 1807-1907, 1907
Newbigging, Thomas. *History of the Forest of Rossendale,* 1868 & 1893 editions
Newspapers:
   Bacup and Rossendale News;
   Bacup Chronoicle and Rossendale Advertiser, 1855;
   Bacup Echo, 1972-1977;
   Bacup Times;
   Burnley Evening Star;
   Joyful News;
   Rossendale Free Press;
   Rossendale Watchman, 1876
Ogden, James. *Fifty years of Bacup life,* 1902
   William, J. H. editor: *Mount Pleasant Methodist Chapel, Bacup: souvenir of its centenary (1841-1941)*
Ormerod, Milton B. *The parish registers of Newchurch in Rossendale as sources of social and medical history,* 1981
Overend, Frederick. *History of the Ebenezer Baptist Church, Bacup,* 1912
Partington, S. W. *The Toll bars and turnpike roads of Bury and Rossendale,* 1921
Phillips, Ron. *The Rossendale Baptists,* 1990
Pilling, James Vincent. *Pilling family scrapbook, compiled 1968-1975*
Pococke, Richard. *Travels through England 1750-51*
Porter, John. *The Making of the Central Pennines* 1980
Public Religious Census 1851. (Public Record Office HO 129/476 and HO 129/477)
Shufflebottom, Diane. *A Study of Heald Wesleyan Chapel,* 1980
Smith, Jonas. *An Historic sketch of the Ebenezer Sunday School, Bacup . . .* 1886
Stephenson, Henry. *Notebooks* (manuscripts)
Stocks, Leslie A. *The History of John Maden & Son Ltd., 1837-1977,* 1977
Slater's Royal National Commercial Directory of Lancashire, 1876
Taylor, W. Gordon. *Bacupian mills.* 3 vols., unpublished manuscripts 1987-1991
   Bacupian quarries unpublished manuscript, 1991
Thorn Wesleyan Methodist Chapel. *jubilee souvenir, 1872-1922*
Trinity Baptist Church, Bacup: History, 1982
Tupling, G. H. *The Economic history of Rossendale* 1927
Turner, William. *Rit! — the story of the East Lancashire loom-breakers in 1826,* 1992
Victoria County History of Lancashire 1914, reprinted 1966
Webb, Beatrice. *My apprenticechip,* 1938 and 1982 editions
Wesley, John. *Journals,* Standard edition 1938
Whalley, David A. *The Rossendale Slipper Unio, 1895-1927,* 1984
Whitworth Town Council: *illustrated official guide* 1977
Wray, Tom. *The Bacup branch. Ramsbottom — Stubbins — Rawtenstall,* 1985
   The Bacup branch: Rochdale — Facit — Bacup 1989

Index

All figures in italics refer to illustrations

Acre Mill 74
   House 65,84
Accrington 27,86
   Pupil Teachers' Centre . 92
Adam of the Dene 12
Advertisements *125,126*
Ailse o' Fusser's 25
Aitken, James 33
   Thomas 33,34,83,104
Alexander of the Dene 12
Allen,
   brothers 27
   Herbert 27
   Margaret 47
   Thomas 17,*22*
Allen's Motors (Bacup)
   Ltd 27,*124*
Amaranthus, HMS 98,*101*
Amateur Astronomy
   Centre 54
American Civil War 36
Anchor Shelter Housing
   Assoc 112
Anderson, Janet, MP 117
Anglo-Saxon Chronicle 11
Anlaf 11
Anti-Easter Dues Assoc 73
Arcon estate 99,*101*
Arkwright, Richard 33
Ashworth, Richard 16
   Miles (1827-1889) 63,65
   Miles (1849-1924) 65
   Young J. *119*
assassination poster *70*
Assisted Education Act
   1891 91
Athelstan, King 11
Atherton, John 74
Bacup Against Crime action
   group 112
   Aged, Blind & Disabled
     Centre 96,99,111
     Treat *110,111*
   Allotment Holders'
     Assoc 106
   Amateur Dramatic
     Society 104,*108*
   Ambulance Hall ... 106,*109*
   and District Horticultural
     Society 106
   and Stacksteads Estate
     Management Board....112
   and Wardle Commercial
     Manufacturing Co 74
   Auxiliary Bible Society . 68
   Baths 105
   Benefit Building Society...45
   Booth 13
   Board of Health 83
   Borough Council 45,63,
                    84,86,*86*
     Arms *82*,84,115
     Charter of
       Incorporation 84
     Common Seal *82*
     Corporation muck cart
       (song) 85
   Borough F.C. 103
   Hospital Trust
     Council 96
   Housing Acts 45
   Botanical Society 106
   Boundaries 87
   Brick & Tile Company . 97
   British Restaurant 99
   Burial Board 84
   Cancer Research Group...*82*
   Cemetery 66

Central Aid Fund ... *88*,96,
                              101
Choral Society 104
   Union 104
*Chronicle & Rossendale
   Advertiser* 106
Citizen's Advice
   Bureau 99,112
Civic Centre —
   projected *120,121*
   Society 112
Clef Club 104
Club Houses 17,45,46
   Society 45
Coat of Arms *38*
Conservation
   Area 116,*122*
Conservative Co-operative
   Industrial Society Ltd...35
Co-operative Hall 18,96,
                               106
   Society 113
   Store *40*,63,98,99,106
   Corporation 26,65,115
   Credit Union 113
   Cricket Club *102*,103
   Echo 113
   Engine Shed *31*
   Fair 13,47
   Fire Service 48,85
   Floral & Hort Soc 106
   Fold 12,13,26,48
   Football Club 52,*102*
   Friday Club 111
   Golf Club 104
   Handbell Ringers 104
   Health Centre *23*,117
   Heritage Office *123*
   Home Guard 98
   Inner Wheel 112
   Inskip League of
     Friendship 112
   Judo Club 106
   Ladies Choir 104
     Guild 112
   Leisure Hall *81*,106
   Liberal Club 64,93,111
   Library 106
   Local Board ... 25,47,48,52,
                         84,85,*86*
   LDV 98
   Male Voice Choir 104
   Manchester Express
     Service 27
   Market 47,96,113
     Hall 44,47,48,84,85,
                     97,116,*120*
   Mechanics' Hall 106,
                           110,115
     Harmonic Soc 104
     Institute 46,66,84,*88*,
                  89,91,96,103,106
   Methodist Utd Choir .. 104
   Motor Garage *31*
   Natural History
     Society 46,66,106
   Neighbourhood Office . 86
   Old Band 52
   Omnibus Conveyance &
     Livery Stables Co 26
   Orchestral Society 104
   Oxfam shop 112
   Police 85
   Poorhouse 71

   Property Owners'
     Assoc 116
   Public Hall 104
   Rag Market 47
   Railway Station 28,113
   Rochdale Tramway *30*
   & Rossendale News 106
   Rotary Club 111
   Saver Store 117
   School Board 55,*88*,91
   Shoe Company ... 74,77,99,
                               113
   Sick Nursing Society 64
   Skating Rink 104
   Soroptimist Club 112
   Starlite Dancers 112,*114*
   Swimming Club 105
   Temperance Choir 104
   Times 46,74,85,91,106
   Unemployed Workers'
     Allotment Soc 106
     Centre 113
   United Baptist Choir .. 104
   Wall of History 98
   War 'Comforts'
     Association 95,99
     Memorial 96
   Wesleyan Circuit 17
     Sunday School
       Union 17
   Wig & Gown Quartette...104
   WVS 99
Baden-Powell, Robert ... 106
Baines, Edward 90
Baltic Fleet 26
Bands: Bacup Old 52,104,
                               107
   Bacup Schools 104
   Broadclough Old 104
   Change 104
   Goodshaw 58
   Home Guard 98
   4th Lancashire Rifle
     Volunteers 104
   Irwell Spring 52,53,*58*,
                            86,104
   Maden recreation
     ground 104
   St John's Church 104
   2nd Rossendale
     Scouts 106,*114*
   Stacksteads *58*,74,*81*,
                            95,104
   Tunstead Boy's Church...74
   Wellington *104*
Bankside 16,45,63,104
Bankhouse 46
Baron, Daniel 63
Baxter's Brewery *79*
Beaconsfield Conservative
   Club 74
Beech House 37
Beer Act 1839 45
Bellac 111
Belle Vue 52,104
Bennet, John 15
Bent 52
Berlin, Battle of 99
Billington, David 105
Birch, Edwin *24*
Blackburn, Hundred of..11,84
Blackburnshire, Forests/
   Chases 71
Blackpool 27,106

Blackthorn Estate 99
Blue Ribbon Union 17
Bocholt 111
Boggart Foundry 73
   Hole Clough 73
Bolton, David 90
   Herbert 63
   & Rochdale District 18
Booth, Joseph 89
Boston 13
Bracewell, Arthur 55
Brandwood ... 13,54,66,84,85
   Lower End 71
   Moor 64,65
   Quarry 28
   Survey 54
Brett, John 34
Brickfield *23*
Bridge, Richard 63
Brigantia 11
Brigg Clough Poorhouse . 71
Bright, John 83
Brightsea Island 106
Britannia .. 27,28,*49*,54 *et seq*,
                            61,84,98
   Coconut Dancers of
     Bacup 55,74,105,*109*
   Greenway 55
   railway station 55,*60*
   sidings 28
   Trough Gate 25,28,*61*
   United FC 56
   Women's Institute 56
British and Foreign Bible
   Society 64
   School Society 90
Broadclough 64,84,86
   Dikes 11,*14*
   Estates 15
   Hall *14*,45,72
Brocklehurst, Albert 115
Brookes Studio 117
Broughton 52
Brun, river 11
Brunabur(g)h, Battle of ... 11
Brynbella 93
Buckingham Palace 113
Burnley 11,26,86
Burton's Corner 26
Bury Masco Industries ... 113
*Busy Body & Rossendale
   Critic* 106
Byron, Lord 54
Capella House 53
Cartwright, Edmund 33
Causeway House 25,54
Cavendish family 65
Central View *94*
Chadwick, Edwin 45,83
   : *Report (Sanitary Condition of
     the Labouring Population,
     1842)* 45,83
   Samuel 72
Chapel Cottages 73
   Villas 53
Chartism 34
Chartists' Room 35
Chase, 'Pa' 106
Chatsworth Park 65
Chester, Constable of 12
Church attendance *22*
   Meadow 93
Churches: Acre Mill 18,74
   Beulah United
     Methodist 55
   Booth Road Primitive
     Methodists 73
   Britannia Wesleyan 55
   Central Methodist 113
   Chapel on the Moors 51
   Christ Church 16,95
   Congregational Chapel....16

128

Deerplay Baptist 51
Doals 53
Ebenezer Baptist . 15,16,17,
    20,106,111,113
Heald Wesleyan 52
Holy Trinity, Tunstead....73
Irwell Terrace . 16,113,115
Mitchel & Crosley Meeting
    House 15
Mount Olivet (formerly
    Gospel Mission) 18
Mount Pleasant
    Wesleyan ... 16,18,*21*,113
Newgate Mission 17
North Street Primitive
    Methodist Church *23*
Old Chapel 53
Orchard Hill (later
    Waterbarn) 72
Particular Baptist 17
Primitive Methodist 16
Providence 18,48
Road End Baptist 72
St John's (Episcopal) Parish
    Church ... 16,*19*,83,*120*
    (new) 18
St Joseph's Mission 18
St Luke's Mission 73
St Mary's Catholic...16,18,*21*
St Nicholas, Newchurch...16
St Saviour's...18,63,65,*67*,69
Salvation Army 104
Shareholders Chapel 16
Sharneyford 53
Stacksteads Wesleyan
    (Methodist) 72
Thorn Wesleyan Chapel..*23*
Tunstead (Holy Trinity)
    Parish Church . 16,*20*,72,
    75,80
Tunstead Mission 73,*77*
Wesleyan Methodist . 72,
    74,*78*
Union Baptist 113
Waterbarn 74
Waterside (Wesleyan
    Methodist Association)
    18,55,113
Zion Baptist 74,113
Churchill, Winston 97,98
Cistercians 12
Clean Air Act 1957 112
Cleaver, Bishop William ... 16
Clegg, Roger 89
    William James 85
Clitheroe Castle 12
    Honor of 12
Cliviser 15
coal mines: Blue Ball 53
    Deerplay 52
    Greave 53
    Hill Top 53
    Old Clough 52
    Old Meadows 36,37
    Stacksteads (The Hile) . 73,
    76
    Tooter Hill 53
Coates, PC Richard 53
Coffee Tavern 17
Co-Houses 35
Collier, John 53
Compulsory Church Rate
    Abolition Act 1868 73
Cooper, A.J. *20*
Co-operative Society 35
Corner 51,52
    Dyeworks 52
Cotton famine 36
    Mills Act 1819 34
    Mill Rules 41
    Spinners' Assoc 105
County Electors Act 1888 .. 85

Cowpe 64,84
    reservoir 46
Cripps, Sir Stafford *88*
Crompton, Samuel 33
Cromwell, Oliver 15
Crook, Lot *23*
Crosley, David 15
Crown Point 25,51
    Post Office 85
Crystal Palace 52,104
Cunliffe, Richard 73
Cuerdale Hoard 11
Danes 11
Darney, William 15,16
Darwen 84,103
Dawson, John 47,84
    Thomas 72
Deansgreave Bridge 55
    Farm 54
Dearden, James 54
Deerplay 15,25,27,46,51
    Hill 51,*58*
    War Memorial *57*
Derby, Lord 52
Disraeli, Benjamin 74
Domesday Survey 11
Dobbs, Kitty *88*
Doorstones 73
District Bank 115
Duckworth, (Sir) James...46,55
    James Ltd 49
Duggleby adze 11
Dykes House Farm 11
Edenfield 86
Edgeside Hall 72
Education Act 1890 91
    1918 90
    1944 93
Edward III 54
Electricity Showroom .. 115
Ellis, Bryan *123*
    George 104
English Heritage 116,117
Elizabeth II, Queen 11
Embassy, The 106
Emily, The 72
Empire Theatre...104,*108*,112
Ewood Bridge 85
Factory Act 1833 90
Facit 27
Fairwell estate 55,112
Falconer, Dr Eric Walter .. 72
    Dr Francis 72
Farholme 86
Farraday, Sgt *70*
Fearns 63,71
    Hall 66,71
Fern Hill Estate 30,72,*80*
    House 72,95
    Military Hospital 72
Fielden, John 34
Finch, John 106
    Lodge 106
Fire engines: *The Irwell* ... 26,
    29,48
    J.H. Lord *100*
    Prince Albert 35,48
Folly Clough 73
Flixton 27
Forest House 108,116
Foster, Willie 105
Fraser, Bishop James 18
Gaskell's 54,113
Gaskell, Thomas 37
Gauxholme 15
Gem Picture Palace 104
Geology of Rossendale 63
George IV 16
    V 52,95
George, David Lloyd 104
Giddy Meadow 13

Gladstone, W.E. 84
Glen, The 55,74,79
    Top 85
Goldthorpe, Ian 116
Goodshaw 16
Gospel Temperance
    Union 17
Gowther Fold 54
Great Exhibition 104
    Harwood 86
Greenend 112
Greens 46,85,86,89
Greensclough 86
Greensnook 16,*19*,89
    Hall 65
Gregory, Fred 55
Grimshaw, Rev William...15,16
'Greetings from t' Top o' t'
    Brow' 99
Halifax 15
Halmot Court 12,71
Hamer, Robert (Bury
    Bob) 72,77
Hamilton, Edward J. 46
Hammerton Green 13,103
Hampson, Thomas *109*
Hardman, Bros 99
    George 99
    Dr William 99,105
Hargreaves, Emma Jane .. 91
    James 33,85,91
Harland, John 26
Hartington, Marquis of...65,84
Hartley, Mary Alice 25
    Police Station 116
Haslingden 11,26
    Grane 63
    Poor Law Union ... 71,85
    & Todmorden Turnpike
    Trust 25
    workhouse 71
Have-A-Go *110*
Haworth, Frank *23*
    'Parson' 73
Heald (Town) ... 15,25,46,51,
    52,90
Healey 27
Health & Morals of
    Apprentices Act 1802 ... 89
Heap, Moses 103
Heap Barn (Farm) 15,53
    Bridge 104
    Hey Farm 53
Heath Hill Estate 80,95
    House 35,72,75
Hebden Bridge 117
Height Barn Farm 65
Hempsteads 13,46,85
    Gardens 96
Henry VII, King 12
    VIII, King 13
Heptonstall 15
Hey Head 54
Heys, Henry (county
    councillor) 86
    Henry (quarrymaster)
    36,55
Heyworth, Anne 65
    Rev James 16,103
    James (town clerk) ... 85,*86*
    Lawrence ... 19,48,*88*,89
Higher Broadclough 51
    Stack 54
    Tunstead 73
Hindle Wakes *81*
Hirst, Rev John 16,*20*
    : preaching chair *20*
Holt, family of Grislehurst...13
    Bros (Rochdale) Ltd 27
    Emily Sarah 65
    James Maden of Stubbylee
    13,63,64,65,*67*,84

    John 24,64,65,73,83
    Judith 64,103
    Richard Durning *88*
    Holt's Siding *32*
    Honey Hole 72,73,76
    Howard & Hargreaves ... 117
    Howarth, Hannah 84
    Howe, Rev John 72
    Howorth, Dick (cricketer)..103
    John 66
    Hoyle, Alice 52
    Edward 17,63,66,*67*
    Harry 98
    Isaac (logo) *37*
    James Henry 104
    John 15
    Joshua (1796-1859) ... 35,
    37,52,63,66,*67*
    (Craven) 66
    & Sons Ltd *38,39*,
    53,66
    Thomas *88*,96,115
Hurstwood 13
Icon Impressions 117
Ingram, driver 26
Illustrated Police News *77*
Isabella 11
Ireland, James 99
Irwell 84,86
    Bank Printworks 74
    Clearance Area 45
    House Farm 51
    River 12,13,26,46,51,64,
    71,84,85,115
    Springs Band 52
    Dyeing Co 52,103
    Football Club 52
    Printing Co 52,53
    Terrace Band of Hope...104
    Valley Walkway *79*
Jackson, John H.
    (engineer) 26
James, Lord, of Tunstead . 15
John, King 11,12
Johnson, John W. 97,99
    Rev William 65
Joyful News 18,*67*
Juliet Bravo 116
Kay, John 33
    John Henry 64
King George V Clock
    Tower *119*
Kirk Gate 15
Knights of St Columba 97
Knowsley Hall 52
Knox, John 15
Kozy Cinema 104
Krazy Kuts 113
Lacy, family 12
    Roger de 11,12,54
Lancashire Life 116
Lancashire Amateur Cricket
    Assoc 103
    Chief Constable 72
    County Council 85
    Footwear Manufacturers
    Association 74
    Rifle Volunteers 104
    Sock Co 54
Lancaster,
    Bomber III JA 913 99
    Duke of 11
    Joseph 90
Lanehead 46
Law, Arthur 47
Lee, Insp William..25,45,83,84
    Lee Farm 11
    letterheads *124*
Limer's Gate 25
Local Government Act
    1888 85
London Relief Committee...34

Lord, & Taylor 114
  John (of Greensnook) ... 33
  John W. 104
Lower Holme 74
  Rockliffe 17
  Tunstead 73
Lumb, John *41*,104
  Valley 25,51
Lytham Regatta 72
MacAdam, John Loudon . 26
McLerie, Jack 37
  James 37
  Samuel 37
Maden, Henry ... 62,63,74,85
  Henry (Hal) 64
  James (1766-1849) .. 35,
                                        64,89
  John (1724-1809) 15,33
  John (1800-1869) 63
  John & Son 63,96
  John Henry (Sir) . 33,*62*,64
  Judith 64
Maden & Ireland 37,99
  Public Baths 64
  Recreation Grounds . 64,104
  Scholarship 63
Manchester & District
  Housing Assoc 117
maps:
  Bacup town centre
    1891 .... *32*
  Britannia 1911 .... *60*
  OS 1892 .... *118*
  Saxton's Lancashire
    1557 .... *10*,13
  Sharneyford 1930 .... *59*
  Stacksteads 1935 .... *80*
  Tunstead & Wolfenden
    1833 .... *75*
  Weir 1912 .... *56*
Marks & Spencer: Penny
  Bazaar 48,*49*,99,113
Marlow, Joyce 97
Mary, Queen 95
Mawdsley, James 55,105
Maxim, James L. 55
Maydin, James 64
Melba, Dame Nellie 64,*69*
Meller, Bill 123
Metropolitan Colportage
  Assoc. 17,22
mills: Acre 74
  Atherton Holme . 74,*77*,*81*,
                                        113
  Beech 35
  Bottom-o-th'-Street 45
  Britannia 54
  Broadclough *41*
  Brooks Bottom 35
  Church Street 33,34,104
  Corn 25,37,117
  Farholme 35,*40*,74
  Flowers 97
  Grove 37,46
  Heap Hey 53
  Height Barn 95
  Holmes 17,36,*82*,*86*,98
  Honey Hole 33
  India 35,36,*38*,113
  Irwell 34,35,45,89,95,96
  Kilnholme 37,*40*
  processes *42,43*
  Lee 36,37,63,105,114
  Lower Mill,
    Rawtenstall *41*
  Midge Hole 35
  New Bacup & Wardle
    Commercial Co 35,*40*
  New Hey 35,113
  Old Clough 34,51
  Olive 37,113
  Park Mill, Britannia 53

Parrock (Park Lumb) 53
Plantation 35,36,*38*,*39*
Ross *31*,36,*38*,*41*
Rossendale 74
  Industrial Co 35
Sharneyford 35,53,91
Spring Gardens .33,35,36,91
Springholme 63
Stacksteads ... 35,36,74,113
Throstle 63
Tong *23*,48,117
Tunstead ...34,55,74,*78*,105
Underbank 33,36
Victoria 74
Warth Mill, Waterfoot .. 26
Waterbarn 34,63,73,90
Waterside 37
Weir 35
Mitchel, William 15
Mitchell, Helen Porter 64
  William 72,103
Mitchellfield Nook 71
  Farm 72
  Workhouse *75*
Moorlands House 66
  Park 66
Mountain, Mrs Zipporah . 86
Mount Pleasant 99
Muggeridge, Malcolm *88*
Mulvaney,
  Rev Henry Joseph 16
Munn, Brothers 52,89
  James 72
  John 35
  Margaret, Alice 72
  Robert 33,34,35,46,
                 48,72,73,83,89
  Robert Angus Law 35
  Robert Whittaker 35,72
Municipal Corporation
  Act 1835 83
Mussidan 111
National Society for the
  Education of the Poor .. 90
New Embassy Bingo &
  Social Club 104
  Regal Cinema 104
Newchurch 15,26,27,28,71
  School Board 90,91
  township of 45,75,84,85
Newgate 13
Newkin (Nookend) 51,98
Nixon, John 112
Nuttall, Walter 52,58,86
Oak House 63
Oakenhead Wood 25
Oastler, Richard 34
Old Clough 52
  Meadows 98
Olivier, Laurence *81*
Olympia Picture Palace 74
Ormerod's Mill 63
  George 72,73
  Lawrence 73
Owens College 63
Particular Baptist Society . 16
Pathfinder Force 99
Patten, John Wilson 83
Penny Post *24*
Pickles Theatre 104
Pikelaw 71
Pilling, Abraham 104
  J.R. 37
Plant Back 47
Pococke, Dr Richard ... 13,15
Poictou, Roger de 11
Porter, Rev William 83
Potter,
  Beatrice ... 17,*19*,48,*88*,117
Premier Skating Rink .. 74,*78*
Priest-booth 53
Priestley, Enoch 90

Lord John 90,106
Public Health Act
  1848 35,47,83
public houses:
  Angel Inn 115
  Barley Mow 54
  Blue Ball (Bull & Dog) . 46
  Britannia Inn 54
  Bulls Head Inn 115
  Deerplay 51,*57*
  Dog & Partridge 55
  George & Dragon
    Inn 25,26,34,
                 45,83,115,*119*
  Hare & Hounds 73
  Hark up to Nudger 45
  Hit or Miss 54
  Holy Lamb 54
  Hop Tree 53
  King George V 115
  Market Hotel 26,45
  Queen's Hotel ..115,*119*,*120*
  Seven Stars 45
  Slip Inn 64
  Spread Eagle, Rochdale ..*24*
  Stag & Hounds 51
  Travellers' Rest 54,55
  Waterloo Inn 46
  Waterworks Inn *50*
  Weir Hotel 52
  Wellington Hotel 55
  Wheatsheaf 53
quarries: Back Cowm 55
  Brandwood 36
  Britannia 36
  Frost Holes 36,72,73
  Greens Moor 36,73
  Hall Cowm 55
  Law Bottom 73
  Head 36
  Lee 36,65
  Rakehead 36,55
Raby's lodging-house 112
Raikes, Robert 89
Rakehead 48
Ramsbottom 84
Rankine, John 52
  Robert 52
Raw Cliffe Wood 63
Rawtenstall 11,26,86
  Shoe & Slipper Co. 37
Reaps Moss 54
Redcliffe-Maud Report
  1969 86
Reddish Carnival *114*
Reform Bill 1832 84
Regal Cinema 112
Rhodes, Ada *82*,86
Ribble, River 11
Riding & Gillow 74
Rigby, William *31*
Riverside 113
Roberts, William 26,34
  W. & Co. *24*
Rochdale & Burnley
  Turnpike Trust 51,54
  parish of 12,71
  Penny Post 26
Pioneers' Equitable
  Soc. 113
  Union 85
Rockett, Walter Samuel .. 105
Rockliffe 84
  House 28,63
  Wood 12
Roclif, Alan de 12
Romans 11
Rooley Moor 25,26,36,72
Rose 'n' Bowl 75,*80*
Rossendale
  Boot & Shoe Exchange . 37
  Borough 86,*116*

Constituency 84
Division Carriage
  Company 26,27
Forest of 11,12,*56*,84
Hunt 52
Players 105
Printing Co 36
Society for visiting and
  instructing the
  blind 18,*23*
Stationery &
  printing works 18
Sunday School Union ... 17
Theatre 104
vaccary 71
Watchman 106
Waterworks Co. 46
Royal Court
  Theatre 64,*69*,104
Royal visit 95,*100*,115
Rule Britannia 54
Sacred Songs for Baptist
  Schools 17
St John Ambulance
  .... 72,95,*109*
St Mary's Players 105
Salford, Bishop of 93
  Catholic Diocese 16
  Hundred 'of 12,65,84
Salute the Soldier Week ... 18
Salvation Army 18
Sandfield 95,*100*
Saunder Clough 53
Saxons 11
Scar End 46
schools: Acre Mill
  Baptist 72,99
  All Saints 93
  Bacup Fold 89
    & Rawtenstall
    Grammar 93,97
  Joint Secondary 92
  Ragged 17,*86*
  Technical 93
  Bethel School 92
  Blackthorn 92,93
  Britannia County
    Primary 55
    Wesleyan 92
  Central Infants 92,*94*
    Junior 92,*94*
    Methodist *110*
  Clegg's Academy 89
  Doals British 91
  Fearns 93,*94*
  Heald Wesleyan 91,92
  Higher Grade 91
  Holy Trinity,
    Stacksteads 93
  Irwell Terrace 91
  Mount Infants 92,93
  Olivet 92
  Pleasant
    Wesleyan 90,91,92
  Newchurch Grammar .. 91,
                                             93
  New Line 90
  Northern 92
  St Ambrose 93
  St John's National 90
  St Joseph's RC 93
  St Mary's RC 90,93
  St Saviour's *62*,92
  Sharneyford 54,90,91
  Stacksteads Wesleyan..91,92
  Thorn 93
  Tunstead 73,93
  Underbank 104
  Waterbarn 91,92,96
  Wesley Place 92,93
  Western 92,93
  Schofield's 74

Sedges 71
Sharney Brook 84
Sharneyford 15,25,27,51,
  53 et seq,64,84,91,98
  : *Saturday Times & Change
  Leader* 54
  Toll Bar House *59*
Shawforth 55,64
Shelton, Arthur *126*
Shepherd, George (Holmes
  Villa) *82,85*
  George (Shepherd's
  Tent) 17
  James 17
Shuttleworth, James 85
Siddall, Richard
  (quarrymaster) 36,73
Siddall's Quarries 28
Sieber, Charles Henry 52
Sissclough 72
Sisters of the Good
  Shepherd 112
Smith, Rev Jonas 18
  Robert *23*
Sowclough 71,72
Spotland, township of 45,
  84,85
Springfield Court 112
Spring Gardens 93
Spurgeon's Child Care ... 112
Stacksteads .... *49*,71 *et seq*,
  97,98,114
  Conservative Club 74
  Defence Corps 95
  Flyer (Tally-Ho) 28
  Liberal Club 74
  Literary Institute 74
  population 17
  railway station . 28,72,73,*79*
  recreation ground 96
  ward 86
  Wesleyan prize choir . 104,
  107
Stanlowe 54
Stansfield, Alan 20
  steam car *30*
Stewart, Robert 89
Stoney Hill 76
Storey, Jack 98
streets: Alma Street 74
  Angel Street 48
  Ash Street 95
  Back Irwell Street 46
  Bacup Old Road 51
  Bankside Lane 117
  Bank Street 48,115
  Bath Street 117
  Booth Road (Old Road)...25,
  27,73,76
  Brick Street 36
  Bridge Street . 26,48,*49*,115
  Burnley Road (Church
  Street) ... 16,17,26,36,*57*,
  98,104,111,115
  Clough Terrace 52
  Coal Pit Lane 36
  Cooper Street 40
  Crey Bottoms 117
  Crown Point Road 57

Dale Street 93,116
Dandy Row 34,104
Earnshaw Road 113
Elgin Street *4*,117,*123*
Forge Street 36
Foundry Street 36
Garden Street 46
Glenborough Avenue ... 97
Goose Hill Street 111
Greensnook Lane 112
Harrow Stiles Lane 51
Herbert Street 74,*78*
Holme Street 73
Industrial Place ... 116,117,
  123
Irwell Street 117
  Terrace 72,116
King Street 112,114
Lanehead Lane .. 16,25,33,
  106,115
Lee Street 115,116
Limer's Gate 51
Lord Street 117
Maden Road 34
Market Street *3*,16,37,45,
  47,48,*49*,*50*,85,90,111,
  116,*120*,*121*
Moorlands Terrace 66
New Line 27,54,55,106
Newchurch Road 104
Oaken Close 112
Old Road 25,73
Park Row 34
Pennine Road 112
Pippin Street *50*
Plantation Street 47,*50*,
  108,111
Quarry Street 36
Rochdale Road .. 25,26,35,
  55,64,104,116
Rook Hill 73
Rose Street 117
St James Square 48,115
  Street 26,*100*,115,*120*
St John's Court *109*
Sieber Row 52
Smith Brow *23*
South Street 73
Step Row 15,51
Stewart Street .. 48,115,*120*
Sutcliffe Street 55
Temple Court . 45,113,*121*
Todmorden Old Road . 15,
  25,53
  Road 54,116
Tong Lane 25,91,117
Treacle Row 52
Trough Gate 25
Tunstead Lane 25
Underbank 40
Union Street 17,116
Wesley Place 66
Yate Street 55
Yorkshire Street 26,46,
  48,115,117,*119*
Strict & Particular Baptist
  Choir 18
  : programme *22*
Stubbins 27,86
Stubbylee Farm 54

Hall *24*,28,65,*67*,86,96,
  98,103,*114*
Park 64,65,66,93,115
Summerseat 35
Sunnycrest 112
Sutcliffe, James Smith 37,
  66,*67*,85
  shop *100*
Sutton, Ernest 99
  E. & Sons 99,113
Syke Foundry 73,74
Tattersall, Ben 98
Taylor Holme Industrial
  Estate 77,*81*
  James 89
Temperley, Thomas 53
Temple, Archbishop
  William 93
Ten Hours Act 1844 103
Thanksgiving & Safety
  Week 98
Thieveley Pike *56*
Thorn 35,98
  House 112
  Meadows 92
Thrutch (Gorge) 26,85
  Tunnel 28
Todmorden Corporation . 27
  Bus 115,*119*
  Edge South 15
  Penny Post *24*,*26*
Tollbar Business Park 113
toll bars: Britannia 25,*60*
  Broad Clough 25
  Deerplay 25,51,57
  Height Barn 25
  Rockliffe 25
  Sharneyford 25,*59*
  Stacksteads 25
  Swan Bar 25
  Tong 25
  Tunstead (Four Lane Ends)
    .... 25,72,*80*
  Underbank 25
Tong 54,84,85,86
Tong(u)e Meadow 18
Top o' th' Bank 64
Tooter Hill 54
Townhead ... 66,115,*119*,*120*,
Towneley, Agnes 13
  John 13
Trippier, David A. 117
Troy Silver Mining
  Company 37,63
Trough Gate Farm 54
Tunstead 71,84,91
  Bottom 73
  coconut dancers
    (troupe) 74,76,105
  Men's Institute 73
  Poorhouse 71
  vaccary 12
Tunstead 12
Turnbull & Stockdale 74
Turner, (forger) 34
Tyne, William John 18
Uttley, Rev John 16
Valley Supply Company ... 74
Vickers, John 105
Victoria, Queen 18,63,65,

71,95,103
Station 97
Vikings 11
Waddington, William 115
Waggoner Tunstead 71
Walmsley Farm 54
War Disposals Board 27
Weapons Week 98
Warship Week 98,*101*
Waterbarn 86
  Band of Hope 74
Waterfoot 18,26,51,84
Waterside Amateur Operatic
  & Dramatic Society .. 104
Webb, Sidney *19*
Weekes, Everton de
  Courcy 103,114
Weir ..... 27,51 *et seq*,*56*,90,98
  Bottom 52
  & District War
  memorial 53,*58*
  Post Office 53,*58*
  United FC 53
  Women's Institute 53
Wesley, John 15,16
Westhoughton Band
  Contest 74
West View 52
Whalley Abbey 12,54
  Abbot 71
  Vicar of 73
Whitaker, Clough 11
  family 45
  James 83
  John 15
  Justice 16,*19*,72
Whitefield, George 15
Whitehead, Caroline 93
  David, & Sons *41*
Whitworth 28,54,84,86
  Doctors 64,89
  UDC 55
  Valley 95
Whitworth Vale Motor
  Omnibus Company
  Ltd 27,29
Whyttacior, James 13
  John 13
  John (2) 13
Wilde, Israel 34
Wilkinson, John F. 91
William I, the Conqueror .. 11
Wilson, Harold 116
Windsor Castle 113
Windy Bank 25,51,72
Wings for Victory Week..98,99
Winsley Hall, Shrewsbury
  .... *14*,*19*
Wolfenden Booth 71,72
Woodhouse, William 47
Woolworth, F. W. 115
Workers' Education
  Association 93
Working men's clubs:
  Britannia 54,55
  Stacksteads 75,*80*
Worrall, Dr Joseph
  Hardman .. 46,66,69,83,84
Worsley Cup 103
Yelloway Motor Services
  Ltd 27

ENDPAPERS — FRONT: Bacup centre, 1851. (The streets in the vicinity of North Street Primitive Methodist Chapel were built in Brickfield in 1855 and are drawn on). BACK: Club Houses, 1862

131

Subscribers

1 Rossendale Borough Council
2 Lancashire County Council
3 Lancashire County Library
4 Bacup Library
5 Bacup Natural History Society
6 Janet Anderson MP

7 Ken Bowden
8 Robert Cecil
9 Clive & Carolyn Birch
10 Margaret Oanester
11 Clifford Heyworth
12 C.M. Crowther
13 John Warley Mitchell
14 L. Askew
15 Rachel Kenyon
16 Edna Wilkes
17 S.A. Tracey
18 Maureen Howarth
19 T. Roper
20 S. Bradley
21 R.B. Knights
22 M. Hodgkinson
23 Michael Kenyon
24 Graham O'Connor
25 J. McWicker
26 D. Fowkes
27 Street Museum Trust
28 S. Brooke
29 John W. Johnson
30 M. Morley
31 H. Dutton
32 Janet Eaton
33 James E. Howarth
34 V. Hitchen
35 Carol A. Whaley
36 A. Johnson
37 Stephen C. Oldfield
38 Councillor K. Boyden
39 Brenda Edwards
40 Marion Finch
41 D. Broadhurst
42 B. Ashworth
43 Peter Brown
44 Pat O'Diorne
45 Andrew Carr
46 D.J. Duerden
47 J.H. Earnshaw
48 Mary Elizabeth Howarth
49 Peter Heyworth
50 V. Ellingworth
51 Sandra Harrison
52 Ralph Nuttall
53 Arthur Giddings
54 N. Jackson
55 Ronald Redfern
56 G. Pickup
57 John B. Taylor
58 Irene Johnson
59 J. W. Doherty
60 P. Sidlow
61 Jean Jackson
62 G. Clarke
63 Richard Pilling
64 S. Connor
65 Eva Clegg
66 Susan Brooks
67 Kathryn Mills
68 D. Gaughan
69 B. Stott
70 Mary L. Hindle
71 T. Bayliss
72 A. Harrison
73-75 V.B. Balshaw
76 P. Kennedy
77 Mary Pounder
78 Mrs J. Humphreys
79 Vincent Turner
80 Brenda Gibbins
81 Frank Ives
82 James Neil Caygill
83 David Clegg
84 Julie Haslam
85 F. Cooney
86 K. Pickup
87 J. Laycock
88 V. Costelloe
89 E. Hollowood
90 S. McCafferty
91 T.A. Liddle
92 Chris Worswick
93 A.J.W. Gill
94 S.K. Carter
95 P.G. George
96 Harry O'Neill
97 K. Simpson
98 J.H. Hall
99 Janet Coyle
100 Peter Leonard
101 Patricia Howarth
102 A. Netherwood
103 Mrs B. Caine
104 S. Anderson
105 Mrs W. Rome
106 Rev M. Holt
107 Judith Rothwell
108 Maureen Wild
109 G. Selby
110 Joan Spencer
111 A. Bibby
112 Eric Ormerod
113 C. Etherington
114 D.S. Farrington
115 H. Greenwood
116 Henry A. Howard
117 Mrs E. Hargreaves
118 Dorothy Brassington
119 Alan Gledhill
120 John & Carol Davidson
121 J. Butterworth
122 A. Bischtschuk
123 R. Harrison
124 V. Bischtschuk
125 Mrs S. Cruise
126 Kevin Butterworth
127 Richard Harris
128 Norman Taylor
129 David Russell
130 Douglas Hardman
131 Jeffrey Lord
132 A. Clegg
133 R.A. Collinge
134 Alfred Humberston
135 Tom Lord
136 James Parkinson
137 Neal Brookes Nuttall
138 G.A. Bolton
139 C.M. Crowther
140 Clifford Heyworth
141 Olive Whitbread
142 Stanley Hall
143 Keith Brennand
144 Thomas Healey
145 Mr & Mrs S. Wright
146 Mr & Mrs E. Cook
147-149 Alan Spencer
150 Tricia K. Barnfield
151 Peter Fisher
152 A. Whitbread
153 Stephen Green
154 E. Gaskell
155 Janet Wilson
156 K.G. Buckler
157 J.H. Nuttall
158 F.A. Robertson
159 F. Taylor
160 S. Hodson
161 R.E. Shepherd
162 D. Smith
163 J. Lee
164 S. Birtwistle
165 W.E. Oldham
166 Grace Stansfield
167 Gladys Lord
168 Doreen Hardman
169 K. Morley
170 Brenda Lord
171 Mr Tomlinson
172 Stephen Lord
173 Thomas Alan Law
174 K. Hayhurst
175-177 David Edmondson
178 R. Ratcliffe
179 Michael Batt
180 Melvin Ormerod
181 M.O. Doyle
182 A. Smith
183 Margaret Dew
184 Brian Whitelegg
185 C.M. Corkhill
186 J. Richardson
187 W. Wright
188 Barbara Hargreaves
189 D.T. Flynn
190 Adrian Nuzzo
191 L. Wright
192 Helena Barton
193 W.M. East
194 L. Corey
195 T. Rourke
196 W. Pilling
197 Peter Duerden
198 Joyce Harker
199 S. Lord
200-201 C.L. Barton
202 Bradley Stott
203 Sharneyford C.P. School
204 Brenda Nichols
205 John Collinge Greenwood
206 C.A. Lovell
207 Michael P
208 Colin W. Cook
209 Mary K. Whitworth
210 David Dale
211 E.F. Smith
212 Mary Pauline Driver
213 Michael Morley
214 M. Darcy
215 Patricia Trickett
216 T.N. Mitchell
217 Julie Bannister
218 Mr Ingham
219 J. Hanson
220 Leonard Pilling
221 Fred Nuttall
222 D. Bennett
223 T.A. Anderson
224 T. Thirde
225 K.A. Hall
226 Hilary A.B. O'Connor
227 R. Gill
228 B. Ashworth
229 Ann Melia
230 Edith Downing
231 V. Spencer
232 Olive Robins
233 Roger Butterworth
234 Margaret Ormesher
235 Derek Fletcher
236 M. Lord
237 S. Johnson
238 Doreen Nuttall
239 E. Taylor
240 H. Francis
241 Russell Helm
242 D. S. Goodbrand
243 J. Walsh
244 A. M. Flanagan
245 R. Coltman
246 E. Grimshaw
247 Richard Smith
248 Frank Dust
249 Herbert Horsfall
250 Evelyn Whittaker
251 R. Lord
252 H. F. Schofield
253 D. Connell
254 M. Walker
255 F. Galliers
256 A. Bibby
257 Doreen Earnshaw
258 Albert & Clive Lord
259 Mr Foden
260 C. Ormrod
261 Sheila Pearson Jones
263 Andrew Horsfall
264 Lynne Marsh
265 David Pilking
266 M. Daley
267 A. Jackson
268 Mr A. Bladwin

(Remaining names unlisted)

132

FROM NEWCHURCH (TURNPIKE ROAD)

KING STREET

CARD[IE] STRE[ET]

IRWELL STR[EET]

RIVER IRWELL